RIES

RETURNING MATERIALS:
Place in book drop to
remove this checkout from
your record. FINES will
be charged if book is
returned after the date
stamped below.

MAR 31 89

400 D072

MICHIGAN STATE UNIVERSI
LIBRARY

FEB 07 2010

WITHDRAWN

D1349910

EDUCATION AND THE CHALLENGE OF CHANGE

A recurrent education strategy for Britain

Ray Flude and Allen Parrott

Foreword by Lord Briggs

LIBRARY
Michigan State
University

Education and the Challenge of Change

**The Open University Press Series
in Adult and Continuing Education**

General Editors:

H. A. Jones   Vaughan Professor of Education,
                   University of Leicester

G. Normie   Special Assistant to the Vice-
              Chancellor, The Open University

Other titles in the series:

Philosophical Concepts and Values in Adult Education,
   K. H. Lawson

The Education of Adults in Britain
   (in preparation) C. D. Legge

Education and the Challenge of Change

A recurrent education strategy for Britain

Ray Flude and Allen Parrott

The Open University Press
Milton Keynes

The Open University Press
12 Cofferidge Close, Stony Stratford,
Milton Keynes MK11 1BY, England

First published 1979

Copyright © Ray Flude and Allen Parrott 1979.
All rights reserved. No part of this work may be
reproduced in any form, by mimeograph or any
other means, without permission in writing from
the publisher.

Made and printed in Great Britain by
Hunt Barnard Printing Ltd, Aylesbury, Bucks.

LC
5256
·G7
F58

British Library Cataloguing in Publication Data
Flude, R
    Education and the Challenge of Change.
    1. Continuing education – Great Britain
    I. Title   II. Parrott, A
    374   LC5256.G7

ISBN 0 335 00257 9

Contents

For Fred, Jane and Oliver

Foreword

This important book presents a lucid and forceful exposition of the case for educational provision to meet the wants and needs of a whole life span.

It draws on all the available literature, foreign and international as well as English, without yielding to fashion or rhetoric. In this context, alas, England is behind a number of other countries in thinking and feeling. Yet at the same time there is much in our distinctive educational inheritance upon which to draw. We have shown, too, that we are capable of effective educational innovation.

I do not agree with all the interpretations in this book – of the past and present role of the universities, for example – but such disagreement in no way detracts from my view that the case advanced in this book is a convincing one which deserves to be widely understood. It is relevant for all kinds of teachers – not just for people professionally involved in education.

I hope that it will be read by administrators and politicians also. The tendency to think that all we need to do to develop 'lifelong education' is to add to existing provision is wrong. We will need to rearrange patterns and to redeploy resources. At a time when there are so many pressures, financial and otherwise, on the existing system, we may be forced to think afresh.

The authors, I believe, have the right values. They proclaim their strong belief, not shared by all administrators and politicians, in learning for its own intrinsic satisfactions. Such a belief should encourage action not retreat.

Asa Briggs
20 June, 1979

Preface

When Mr Callaghan, in answer to pressure from many quarters, announced a 'Great Debate' on education in 1976, the topics put forward were almost entirely restricted to the period of compulsory schooling for children. This automatic equation of education with schooling revealed a major national weakness and lack of insight. Tinkering with schools will not produce an education system which can satisfy the requirements of this country in the latter part of the twentieth century. Both the educational demands of individuals and those of industry would be better served by a system which encompasses the whole of life. Such a perspective must eventually transform our approach to education. Nowadays teachers can only resist pressures from employers for more strictly relevant educational experiences because they believe that they have only a relatively short period in which to transmit their version of our accumulated wisdom and civilization. Equally it is only possible for employers to resist the demand for paid educational leave because they, too, have been conditioned to think of education as a childhood activity. The answer to many problems in British education lies in some form of recurrent education system which would enable all individuals to build throughout life on the foundations laid in a childhood period of compulsory education.

Unfortunately, ideas about recurrent education in Britain have become largely a matter for theoretical study – a concern of detached academics and non-resident 'eurocrats'. It is essential to look practically at the arguments in favour of a recurrent system and at the kinds of institutional forms which it might take.

This book is an attempt to formulate such a practical

viewpoint. Both the products of education systems and the systems themselves have to live in the real world. We are not concerned with utopias or revolutions, and, therefore, if we are to see the development of a recurrent system in Britain, it will be necessary to convince all sectors of the community that the scheme is a valuable advance. Consideration of these issues is well timed, as the pressures of social and technological change increasingly conflict with the individual's desire for stability and security. For example, it is being suggested, with some degree of desperation, that since the introduction of micro-processors will bring about another 'industrial revolution' a programme of education and training must be devised to help people cope with them. But this kind of management as a reaction to 'crisis' is precisely the kind of response which a developed recurrent education strategy would hope to avoid. All of us have to be geared up to expect such changes as a matter of course. There can be no such thing as the last change. The most important technological revolution is always the next one. It is also being predicted that surplus capacity will become available at various points in the education system in the final decades of the century. It is imperative that such surplus capacity is used for the development of a recurrent system.

The key themes which recur through this book could provide the guidelines for such development. First, in addition to a commitment to lifelong opportunities for study, the British education system must reject the existing division between learning and earning. It must have broad as well as long perspectives. Second, a successful recurrent education system cannot be created without influencing the compulsory schooling of the young. It cannot merely be an addendum to the existing school system. Third, a recurrent education system must itself be a learning system. Its institutions must be able to adapt flexibly to the changing requirements of individuals and social organizations. Fourth, and perhaps most important, the seeds of such a recurrent education system already exist in Britain and could be developed without either massive upheaval or expenditure.

Each of these themes will be new to many people; none is so well known or understood that all its implications have been fully worked out. Inevitably, therefore, there is some repetition of ideas as we attempt to create a total picture of recurrent education in theory and practice, and to make it accessible to a wide audience. In time the ideas in this book will not need to be repeated. They will have become part of the popular consciousness. But as yet they are hardly even part of academic debate. The patterns of work, of social change and of existing forms of education in Britain must bring them into the public arena well before the end of the century.

Ray Flude
Allen Parrott
1979

Chapter 1

Recurrent Education: the Idea

In October 1975 the newly-formed Association for Recurrent Education discussed a draft document which included the following sentences:

> Recurrent education constitutes a comprehensive educational strategy including all levels of educational provision. Its essential characteristic is the distribution of educational opportunity throughout the lifespan of the individual. It allows the alternation of periods of structured educational experience with work, leisure and retirement. It is to be regarded as an alternative to the traditional pattern of educational provision in which the majority of formal education is experienced in the first twenty-five years of life. Its acceptance will require a reconsideration of every facet of existing educational provision . . . Its goal is the learner with greater autonomy better equipped to participate in the continuous shaping and re-shaping of his or her environment and society.[1]

The whole of this book can be seen as an attempt to amplify and refine this valuable brief definition of recurrent education. The rest of this chapter fills out the ideas incorporated in recurrent education and introduces themes which will be more thoroughly explored in later chapters.

Recurrent education can be described as having a vertical and a horizontal dimension. The vertical dimension consists of the notion of opportunities for periods of planned learning *whenever* the need is recognized throughout the length of life. The horizontal dimension consists of the notion of opportunities for periods of planned learning *wherever* the need is recognized throughout the breadth of life.

The implications of the vertical dimension go beyond the mere extension of adult education opportunities. In a system of recurrent education there would be no need to regard the education of adults as their 'second chance' or their 'compensation' for earlier omissions. Education would not be provided as a solid block in the early years with scattered and unco-ordinated opportunities to 'top-up' or 're-sit' in adult life. Present distinctions in concept between 'education' on the one hand and 'adult education' on the other would become meaningless. It would be the most natural thing in the world for anyone to start learning anything at any age, and while a person's age might provide some guidance as to *how* he or she would be taught, it would not be a condition of *whether* he or she should be taught. The task for the initial period of education would be preparatory, providing young people with the basic tools for a life in which recurring periods of learning were to be regarded as normal. Comprehensiveness would be provided by the education system as a whole, not merely by its 'front end' in childhood.

The significance of the horizontal dimension is that it cuts right across existing educational barriers and into areas of life where the usefulness of education provision has been either unrecognized or ignored. One of the main concerns of this book is the connection of education with the world of work, but family life, citizenship and community involvement are examples of other areas of life which are full of possibilities for recurrent education, as well as leisure and retirement mentioned in the extract above. A recurrent education strategy develops the educational possibilities across a wide range of life; it works towards a world in which education plays a more meaningful part in people's lives and, as a corollary, a world in which lives are made more meaningful through education.

'Recurrent education' as used in this book is therefore a

shorthand term for the ugly phrase 'a system of co-ordinated, recurrently provided opportunities for structured forms of learning throughout, and concerned with, the whole of life'.

Unfortunately, there is no generally accepted term for the ideas incorporated in what we call 'recurrent education'. The Association for Recurrent Education has chosen to follow the Organization for Economic Co-operation and Development in using the term, whereas other organizations and writers have preferred a variety of different names for very similar, though not necessarily identical, thoughts about educational futures. 'Lifelong education' is the preferred usage of UNESCO, while the Council of Europe has mainly used the term 'permanent education' as a direct translation of the French *l'education permanente*. Many writers have used different terms altogether, including 'continuing education', 'lifelong integrated learning' and even the opposite of recurrent, 'continuous education'.

It would be tedious to chart in detail this semantic jungle, but because it causes confusion the position adopted in this book must be made clear from the start. Neither 'lifelong' nor 'permanent' convey the right message in English. The terms 'lifelong education' and 'lifelong learning', used interchangeably in the highly influential Faure Report (published by UNESCO in 1972 under the evocative title *Learning to Be*),[2] have come to possess more inspirational than practical value. In English the adjective 'permanent' contains an unfortunate ambiguity, having connotations of ineradicable ink stains which are more or less opposite to what is intended by 'permanent education'. 'Recurrent education' seems to provide the phrase least likely to be feared or misunderstood, for 'lifelong' also has some unpleasant associations in English with prison sentences and funeral notices. Furthermore, the word 'recurrent' does incorporate more precisely than any other adjective the central idea of alternating, at intervals throughout life, between educational periods (of varying lengths) and the normal routine activities of life. 'Continuing education', for example, does not convey this notion of alternation at all. Although it is increasingly used to denote all aspects of the education of adults, 'continuing education' might more usefully be confined to the immediate post-school education of young people, after the lengthy compulsory period and before the start of those recurring opportunities, usually of shorter duration, envisaged for mature adults.

However, language usage is seldom significantly modified by the force of rational argument. Even among those who write about 'recurrent education' there is no unanimity on the nature of the concept. Recurrent education has itself often been used to describe the adult part, the post-school sector, of a proposed 'lifelong' or 'permanent' education system. The OECD, in its clarifying document on the topic, assumes the major concerns of recurrent education to lie in post-school reforms with only an 'indirect effect' on existing school systems, whereas this book assumes the radical and direct effect of recurrent education throughout the educational system.[3] A group of essays published in 1974 under the title of *Recurrent Education* displayed some widely varying viewpoints about goals and strategies among its authors.[4] There is therefore no possibility that either the concept of recurrent education, or the words in which it is couched, will survive the trip to reality unaltered by debate or circumstances. A work such as this aims to contribute to the debate and to point to some of the circumstances. It may well be that some term other than 'recurrent' will eventually be preferred and become the accepted phrase in the language for a similar set of ideas to those outlined in this book.

This lack of unanimity about terms has encouraged sceptics to dismiss all the ideas embodied in these concepts as woolly, indefinable and therefore not worth bothering about. It is very easy to be sceptical about the reality of recurrent education, to claim that it lacks a conceptual framework, or that it cannot be studied through empirical observation. Unfortunately for critics, it is much less easy to deny the reality of glaring educational problems in our society. It is just as escapist to dismiss recurrent education on the grounds of its vagueness as it is to embrace the concept uncritically as a heaven-sent panacea for all our educational ills. The importance of recurrent education lies in the problems which it is confronting and to which it is attempting to provide solutions. Problems cannot be wished away just because the ideas and concepts with which we reach out towards an understanding of them are not yet clear in all their implications. While it would be foolish not to recognize the need for greater clarity in dealing with the ideas and practices associated with recurrent education, it is always in the last resort more important to be precise about the formulation of problems than about the exact meanings of words used to grapple with them. This book attempts to provide a coherent statement about the strategy of recurrent education, its implications and practical possibilities in Britain in the late twentieth century. It is not aimed to be a definitive work of concept analysis.

The essential premise of recurrent education is that it is no longer possible to 'receive' all the education required for life in the period traditionally devoted to education or schooling, say in the eleven to eighteen years after the age of 5. The demands made by the world of rapid change in which we live affect us in all our social roles, though perhaps most obviously in the role of salary or wage-earner. Therefore, there is a need throughout life to apply to education the principle of recurrence, i.e. the planned interruption of the flow of normal social and working life by periods overtly devoted to learning.

A further premise related to a recurrent education strategy is that, even if it were considered desirable to do so, the most affluent society could not indefinitely increase the proportion of national resources devoted to education to the extent that all adults, at any time of their lives, could be given open-ended access to what has traditionally been regarded as further and higher education.

The implied contradiction between these two premises can be resolved by examining existing school and post-school sectors of education, including all kinds of training agencies, both formal and informal, with a view to assessing how far existing provision meets the needs of individuals. It will appear from such an examination that a shift in resources from school to post-school education is both socially and, more important, educationally desirable, and also that there exists a large amount of waste, duplication and spare capacity in the British education and training system. A recurrent education system need not involve a vast increase in the costs of education provision. If secondary schools were to reconsider their role and, if arbitrary distinctions between education and training were dropped, total existing resources of plant, of expertise and of cash could be adjusted and redistributed to meet the real learning needs of individuals.

One of the simplest ways to appreciate the need to overhaul present educational structures is to look closely at every type of education, every institution and every course and to consider the questions 'what is being taught, and why?' As a result of this questioning many people will accept the existence of serious educational problems. Educational goals are confused, linked in mysterious ways with employment chances and policies of social equality, and courses are multiplied without seeming to relate to any goal at all save that of obtaining a certificate, which itself may or may not prove useful in the outside world. Many people will find the case for reform proven, yet find the proposed alternatives altogether unbelievable.

A major reason why recurrent education and associated concepts are sometimes dismissed is that their supporters have claimed too much for them. Frequently these concepts are tied in with a view of some future utopian society with unrecognizable social and economic features. A work such as *Learning to Be* proclaims its vision of lifelong education with flair and imagination but it has little value for those who have to devise policy in the real world.[5] But it is at least more readable than those documents emanating from international organizations in which, for the sake of consensus among nations of widely varying political aims and structures, educational goals are expressed in bland, vague generalizations full of the kind of jargon which Dore has characterized as 'Unospeak'.[6]

A much less anodyne approach, yet one which also provides fuel for critics, is to assume revolutionary goals for new forms of education – goals connected with the transformation of social and political reality. Ken Richardson proclaims the need for a 'recurrent education paradigm', yet finds it 'inappropriate to define the forms recurrent education would take' on the grounds that the 'fostering of learning in real life contexts will engender a changing polymorphism that would always defy description'.[7] If a system of recurrent education is to provide the way ahead, the attempt must be made from the start to define its probable forms and to match them to clearly stated goals. Moral exhortation, arid generalization and wishful thinking will not advance the cause of recurrent education. Recurrent education cannot be allowed to settle forever in the realm of good intentions.

In this work, therefore, the example of the OECD has been followed and recurrent education treated as a realistic strategy rather than a state of mind or a metaphorical call to arms. There is no need to posit dramatic reforms in social and economic arrangements as a precondition of recurrent education, nor need such reforms be expected as a direct result. Recurrent education is a strategy for reform and not a recipe for utopia. It has a close relationship with other social and economic policies under consideration, chiefly perhaps industrial democracy, but it is not dependent on them. Its most radical goals relate to individual learners, not to social groupings, and to present realities at least as much as to future possibilities. Its development should be the task of realistic men of vision, not of idealistic visionaries. Even the OECD, and in particular one of its most influential contributors, Torsten Husen, places too much emphasis on the goal of social equality.[8] Egalitarianism is seen as an essential aim of recurrent education instead of as a desirable political goal towards which recurrent education might provide one effective set of means.

It is important to be clear about this. One can start with a belief that educational arrangements in Britain both reflect and help to perpetuate a society with faults and inadequacies. One can believe that a system of recurrent education would not only benefit individual learners but help to improve this society, not least by providing genuine substance to that clichéd educational promise of all political parties – equality of opportunity. One can believe, with an OECD report, that in recurrent education schemes 'those with low incomes and little previous schooling should receive preferential treatment'.[9] Yet such beliefs put recurrent education into a democratic and humane context (which is certainly where it belongs); they do not help to define or expound the concept or its goals. All the evidence from the American education projects with minorities in the 1960s shows that it is unrealistic to expect anything more than benefits to individuals from educational campaigns.[10] By focusing its main concern on individuals – on all individuals at any age and at any stage in life – recurrent education ought to achieve a degree of genuinely comprehensive education not yet conceived. Many profound changes may arise as a result of people's new perceptions consequent upon their new educational opportunities, but then again they may not. Fundamental economic, political and social changes, however desirable, are not to be confused with the strategy and goals of recurrent education, even though in practice it will inevitably be linked with economic, political and social forces. To delay educational reform while waiting for reforms in other spheres is as unwise as it is unnecessary. Education systems and the societies in which they operate are related in highly complex ways and not according to a simple cause–effect model.

The left-wing counter-argument, that ameliorative social measures such as those envisaged in recurrent education policies will only help to perpetuate an undesirable capitalist system, is seductive, but on examination it does not impress very greatly. This argument requires an act of faith in Marxist analysis and in the potential leaders of 'the revolution' which is not supported by the evidence of history. But it is necessary to dissociate recurrent education entirely from the charge that it is merely a tool of advanced capitalism, that in its emphasis on work as an acceptable and indeed desirable context for education, it is pandering to the demands of a relentlessly acquisitive, materialistic and uncultured society. Some of the most hostile critics of the strategy of recurrent education will be educationists who, whatever their political views, believe that a recurrent education system will result in the subordination of traditional educational goals, associated with a disinterested love of learning for its own sake, to externally imposed goals associated with learning as a means to material reward.

Nothing could be further from the recurrent education strategy developed throughout this book than the subordination of educational to materialistic values. The need to break down barriers between education and the world of work arises not from a desire to glorify work but in order to praise education, not to help perpetuate 'false consciousness' but in order to give every individual the chance to find his or her own form of personal development inside or outside work. Dewey, who can be regarded as the major philosophical founding-father of the ideas in recurrent education, claimed that genuine education cannot exist for all unless all are free to choose their own particular pattern of growth.[11] For many people, work both creates and expresses the major part of their identity. If we ignore work, therefore, we deny to large numbers of people that creation of self, and development of inner potential for growth, which are fundamental to the traditional goals of education.

To contrast work, as an alienating system of dehumanization, with education, as a life-enhancing system of personal growth, is to foster an exceptionally damaging and crude polarity, and to ignore the perceptions of most of the people engaged in both systems. It is this myth which has ensured that most people regard their work, with all its potential, in terms of time as well as of content, for personal development, as an area of life completely unconnected with their education. It has also, somewhat ironically, ensured that for most people engaged in educational activity the time is so short, and the desire to get into work at the right level so great, that there is little possibility of undertaking learning 'for its own sake'.

The pursuit of academic excellence, the cultivation of critical awareness, the development of heightened sensibilities, the transmission of cultural values – all those aspects of a liberal education which can shape and enlarge a personality – are under no threat from recurrent education. On the contrary, an educational system which sees its province as the whole lifespan, and which provides a network of learning opportunities throughout life rather than a hierarchical ladder at the start of life, would be likely to achieve these aims more effectively and for many more people.

One of the most expensive, and least publicized, 'lies' in the education system is that 18–21-year-olds studying for liberal arts and social science degrees at universities and polytechnics spend a lot of their time exulting in the joys of intellectual discovery. Most of them obtain certificates; some may work hard for them; but only a tiny minority have the slightest acquaintance with the idea of learning for its intrinsic satisfactions. Any Open University Summer School, as well as many more humble adult education experiences, will show that learning for its intrinsic satisfactions still exerts a strong pull but only for those who are ready for it. Far from being hostile to the ideals of liberal education, of the 'educated man', a recurrent education system would stop the need to pay mere lip-service to them.

The idea that the world of work is harsh and impersonal,

using people for productivity and irreconcilable with personal development, finds its administrative expression in the distinctions between vocational and non-vocational, education and training, pure knowledge and applied. Society should discard these categories, which, whatever their previous utility, now merely provide barriers between people and their chance of personal development. The origin of the emphasis which most people, men especially, place on the work aspect of their lives is quite likely to be found in the way other options have been firmly, if unwittingly, closed during their childhood. Options associated with the fundamental creative and expressive elements in education are indissolubly linked with immaturity and with failure. This theme will be explored in greater depth, so it is sufficient here to point out that recurrent education demands that earning and learning be linked together in tandem precisely in order that large numbers of people do not continue to have to find their identity and justification for existence in jobs which are frequently boring and repetitive.

A more optimistic, longer-term and by no means incompatible way of looking at the world of work is to see our age as the start of a post-industrial society in which work, through a creative use of technology, can finally lose its nineteenth-century image of dirt, squalor and exploitation. The industrial revolution and its legacy of mass labour and profit-dominated economies, made Marx's noble vision of work as 'the essential vocation of man, the objectivization of his generic life'[12] a hollow dream. Yet European languages persist in making some distinctions between work and labour, *'oeuvre'* and *'travail'*, *'werk'* and *'arbeit'*. Hannah Arendt has shown how in each case the first-named of the pair retains a link with the heights of human achievement, as in 'works' of art, whereas the second is linked with the unmitigated toil and menial tasks which the Greeks felt appropriate to slaves and animals.[13] It is fanciful perhaps to see post-industrial societies shifting entirely from a 'wage-slave' mentality (*animal laborans*) to a 'worker-craftsman–

director' mentality (*homo faber*); yet it may be that schemes of job enrichment, moves towards worker participation and, especially, policies of recurrent education will turn out to be more than straws in this particular wind.

References

1 *Adult Education*, vol. 48, no. 5, January 1976, p. 343.
2 Edgar Faure, *Learning to Be,* London, UNESCO/Harrap, 1972.
3 Organization for Economic Co-operation and Development (OECD), *A Strategy for Lifelong Learning*, Centre for Educational Research and Innovation (CERI), 1973.
4 V. Houghton and K. Richardson (eds), *Recurrent Education*, London, Ward Lock Educational, 1974.
5 Faure, *Learning to Be* (see note 2 above).
6 R. Dore, *The Diploma Disease: Education, Qualification and Development*, London, Unwin Educational, 1976, p. 105.
7 Houghton and Richardson (eds), *Recurrent Education*, pp. 18–19 (see note 4 above).
8 T. Husen, *Social Background and Educational Career*, Paris, OECD/CERI, 1972.
9 OECD, *Education and Working Life in Modern Society*, Paris, OECD Report, 1975.
10 C. Jencks *et al., Inequality: A Reassessment of the Effect of Family and Schooling in America*, New York, Basic Books, 1972.
11 J. Dewey, *Democracy and Education*, London, Macmillan, 1916; and *Experience and Education*, London, Collier-Macmillan, 1938.
12 Quoted in J. Simpson, *Today and Tomorrow in European Adult Education*, Strasbourg, Council of Europe, 1972, p. 219.
13 Hannah Arendt, *The Human Condition*, University of Chicago Press, 1958, pp. 79ff.

Chapter 2

Recurrent Education and the Challenge of Change

Recurrent education as we conceive it derives much of its force from those new challenges to education systems and attitudes which arise from rapidly changing societies. The aim of this chapter is to explore the nature of these challenges and to emphasize how flexibility lies at the heart of recurrent education and its view of individual development. Present systems of education patently fail to provide the flexibility necessary to cope with the challenge of change. Later chapters will examine how existing institutions of education and training can to some extent be viewed as impediments to recurrent education because they stem from an historical development which has tended to split them apart rather than bring them together. Both education and training are important parts of the process by which members of our society are inducted and initiated into useful and life-forming roles in it. This socialization process takes place in many ways and at all stages in individual development. It is the way in which society recasts itself in its own image. Important aspects of the process take place within those formal institutions which are attempting, to a greater or lesser extent, to create a pattern for the individual's development. Whether the institution is a school or a training establishment, it is concerned with the management of socialization. It should be the task of all forms of organized learning to ensure that the process is as constructive as possible for each individual.

Alvin Toffler's phrase 'future shock' has almost become a cliché in the few years since his book was first published.[1] The phrase has caught the imagination because it so dramatically pinpoints a factor which has recently become a cause of concern. We are caught up in an increasingly rapid flow of technological and other changes which affect our way of life. Despite the simple nature of the phrase and the concept, the problem is complex. The picture is neither as clear nor as desperate as the prophets of doom would draw.

It is possible to draw exponential curves showing the accelerating rate of change which has been, and is being, experienced in such fields of human activity as the growth of speed, the use of energy and the discovery of elements. But such curves give a false picture for our purpose, since these are not all changes which affect individuals directly. It is only when the rate of change speeds up and, more important, the rate at which changes are diffused through society that the issue becomes one of personal adaptation. It is these diffusion and 'use' rates which matter to the individual and change his life. It took over 150 years for the steam-engine to spread broadly throughout the populations of users. The motor-car took forty to fifty years, the transistor about fifteen. How long before the micro-processor becomes a commonplace? The impact of change in history has so far been absorbed with relative ease. Man has coped with technological change from the first point in his evolution at which he began to use simple pebble tools. But we are now living within an industrial system which is keyed into change, research and development as a way of life. It is no longer the case that an inventor makes a breakthrough, and a company either chooses or is formed to exploit it. Industrial firms are continuously involved in research and development, to change both products and means of production. Change is built into the system and innovation comes about as part of an on-going process. Two major examples have been the *Manhattan Project* and *Appollo*, but in the more mundane sphere of international relations, technological innovation is considered the key to economic development and growth; and within the competitive national market-place it is the new product or technique which is the weapon that brings success.[2] We can visualize a total state of flux, caused by increasingly rapid rates of diffusion, and we can foresee man's inability to cope.

Technological change has its most obvious and powerful effect in the world of work. In the past it was usually possible to deal with technological change by creating a new job, taking on young men and training them. Change in work techniques could be fitted within the pattern of men's working lives. A man could expect that the kind of job in which he began his working life would still need to be done when he thought about stopping work. Now, in many fields, the time between radical changes is less than a generation and men are increasingly asked to change their jobs to fit the pattern of change and obsolescence.

There are also major changes in the pattern of the labour market. Jobs are changing as a result of a general shift in emphasis from production to service industries. The majority of the working population is no longer concerned with production. From 1961 to 1976 the proportion involved with service industries grew from 49 per cent to 53 per cent of the working population. This proportion is expected to reach 57 per cent by 1981.[3]

In the small scale how do these changes show up? Let us take an everyday example of the effects of inter-generational change in one industry. The construction industry has seen tremendous change in techniques and materials since the war. The use of power tools and equipment, the influx of new materials and the development of prefabrication, both as complete building systems and for parts of buildings, have all affected the patterns of recruitment and training. Small building firms now find that it is virtually impossible to replace carpenters who were trained fifty years ago and are now retiring. Men are no longer trained to the same set of skills, because the needs of the large firms in the building industry have changed so dramatically. Most of the components which a carpenter used to manufacture to order, to fit the particular problems of each building, are now available, machine-made, 'off the peg'; and the carpenter's job has become one of assembly, or merely the construction of shuttering for concrete. The emphasis for skilled labour has shifted away from the building site to the design of modular components and the establishment of production techniques. As a result, when maintenance or repair work is required which cannot be handled in this way, there is no one who can carry it out. This is perhaps an effect which could have been predicted from the steady line of technological innovation, but there are also sudden and catastrophic changes in employment patterns. The 1973 oil embargo and consequent increase in petrol prices, brought about, at least in part, by the Arab countries' desire to maximize their benefits from a limited resource, led to changes throughout the economy. Employers learned from the 'three-day week' that they could 'shake-out' employees and work a reduced labour force more intensively. We see in 1979 a high level of unemployment and many predictions that there can be no return to 'full employment' of the kind experienced in the 1950s. The same kind of employment catastrophe has been predicted as a result of the introduction of micro-processors. The outcome is as yet uncertain. There are as many who trust that the innovation will stimulate employment as there are those who fear long-term widespread unemployment.

But having recognized the inevitability of change, we have to face the possibility of undisirable changes. When it comes to planning the future the human race is still in the novice stage. One can attempt precise predictions of growth curves or carry out Delphic studies, but fundamentally our ability to plan for the future depends on the ability of key individuals to imagine the future; and individuals, particularly those closely concerned with innovation, are notoriously poor at prediction. Rutherford maintained until his death in 1937 that the atom could not yield exploitable energy.[4] Buckminster Fuller, writing in 1967, considered the possibilities of technological advance: 'the next point for a significant new chapter would be around 1975, nine years from now. What that will be we can only guess at – sending ourselves around the world by radio?'[5] The difficulties of this kind of prediction are enormous and even the work of the Hudson Institute, with its alternative scenarios, cannot expect to cover all the possibilities. As Herman Kahn points out, the social and cultural ramifications of even a clear and simple, predictable technological change defy analysis. Kahn suggests, for example, that a wise man in 1900, thinking about the possible development of privately owned motor-vehicles, might have predicted the end of horse-drawn transport, the growth of the road network, garages and the suburbs, but he would have been unlikely to predict the changes in the sex habits of young Americans that the car made possible.[6]

These are difficulties in predicting the speed of change in technology and in assessing its impact. At the same time we are beginning to query the very value of the straight line of technological development towards the science-fiction utopia. Arthur C. Clarke in *Profiles of the Future*, published in 1962, criticized the failure of nerve shown by those who had not believed in the power of science and technology to solve problems: 'Most of the things that have happened in the last fifty years have been fantastic, and it is only by assuming that they will continue to be so that we have any hope of anticipating the future.'[7] Science as the salvation of mankind has been a great political banner. As Lyndon Johnson put the case in a message to Congress on 15 February 1965, 'The power over nature which science is giving our generation is permitting us to look forward with hope towards the solution of many age-old problems, if we apply the results of scientific advance well and wisely.' But in the 1970s it is being stressed that it is partnership with nature, and not power over nature, which is the way ahead. The optimistic approach which assumed that the 1960s represented an unqualified advance on any previous decade is too simple.

There are few men who find themselves as well placed to judge the potential effects of change as Townsend Harris, the first US Ambassador to Japan. Entering the country in 1856 he watched the first impact of western ways. At the end of his first day, having raised the flag over a ruined temple, he wrote, 'Grim reflections – ominous of change – undoubted beginning of the end. Query if for the real good of Japan?'[8] Most of Harris's contemporaries would not have queried the rightness of the chain of events which led to the rapid industrialization of Japan, but in the 1970s many would doubt the value of, and fear the stresses resulting from, high-speed 'modernization' and 'development' of this type. They would emphasize the values of traditional Japanese culture. In a sense we are talking about a changing 'morality' of change itself, which overlays the question of our ability to bring about change and deal with its impact. Our value judgements about change are uncertain and the 'right' direction for change is unclear. What is clear is that the road of technological development and improvement can no longer be the automatic and obviously 'right' choice. Through our growing understanding of ecology we are beginning to appreciate the interactive nature and the inter-dependence of our problems – problems which will only be solved by a new kind of awareness. We have to develop new ways of living with, and managing, change.

The problems of pollution and man's pressure on the environment present large-scale examples of change. Our constant difficulty is in understanding and coping with innovations and their effects. We cannot react with the conclusion that since innovations create these problems we should have no more innovation. In response to the problem of over-population, for example, can we simply lower our standard of living to subsistence level and merely conserve our present position? A more sophisticated and positive solution is to provide a wider understanding of environmental issues and a deeper awareness throughout the population. This is an educational task. Through education we must develop a learning population which can adapt to changes of all kinds, and which can manage change. The process of adaptation will inevitably involve disruptions at the personal level, since despite the effects of these kind of changes in work patterns, and the widespread recognition of the impact of innovation, our basic personal mythology remains one of stability, and there is tremendous resistance to allowing these changes to penetrate our everyday lives. R. A. Nisbet, the American sociologist, has shown that in their deep underlying structures modern societies are characterized at least as much by persistence as by change.[9] Peter F. Drucker, another American, has also argued persuasively that the fifty years before 1913 were marked by far more significant technological innovation than the fifty years after.[10] This may be so, but it is the cumulative effects of many changes which have become important to us all. As individuals we attempt to retain a stable conception of ourselves against a shifting backcloth. All our upbringing and our experience in schools lead us to expect stability; and yet Nisbet talks of 'the urgent apprehensions of rootlessness, alienation and estrangement in the twentieth-century mind', and Drucker writes of an 'age of discontinuity' now upon us. Today we are experiencing political, cultural and social change, all happening simultaneously. It is the task of an education system to come to terms with an age of discontinuity and to devise constructive learning strategies which will enable people to adapt to changes in their own lives without feeling any threat to the overall integrity of their identity. If education neglects this task, the field is left open for different kinds of solution.

There are already negative reactions to change which show the great stress which the attempt to adapt imposes. The search for new faiths, the nostalgia for the recent past, mysticism and other forms of 'opting out', are all ways of turning away from the challenge of change. Jacob Bronowski, at the end of *The Ascent of Man*, expressed his fear thus:

I am infinitely saddened to find myself suddenly surrounded in the West by a sense of terrible loss of nerve, a retreat from knowledge into – into what? Into Zen Buddhism, into falsely profound questions about, Are we not really just animals at bottom? Into extrasensory perception and mystery. They do not lie along the line of what we are able to know if we devote ourselves to it: an understanding of man himself. We are nature's unique experiment to make the rational knowledge prove itself sounder than the reflex. Knowledge is our destiny.[11]

The British education system still acts on the assumption, legitimate 100 years ago, that it is capable of providing a complete preparation for living, an end-product, the 'educated man'. The Victorian public school prepared young men for a relatively stable world. It has bequeathed us a system of mass schooling which, against the evidence, continues to assume the same degree of stability. The British education system is poorly equipped for even the most basic objectives of helping people to exist and to cope with their problems in a changing world. Yet education ought to be meeting the challenge of change in ways which take people beyond mere 'coping' or 'existing'. By giving people an understanding of their environment, and an awareness of the effects of change, an education system can help them not just to survive but to shape and control their lives. At the same time education, recognizing the human need for psychological stability, for security and a sense of continuity, is also the source of solid mental supports in the face of any psychological disruptions which threaten individuals as a consequence of social change. Education provides the means of developing genuinely strong and lasting supports and of avoiding the sham and the ephemeral in life.

Technology, economics, politics, culture, morality, leisure, community – in every conceivable aspect of modern society change influences us to some degree. Institutions operating in all these fields are influenced by change no less than individuals, and it is educational institutions which provide a crucial yardstick for measuring the effectiveness of a society's response to social change. Today, more than ever before, society can legitimately expect educational institutions to show the way to other organizations, to take a lead in coping with the difficulties of a changing world. Any system of recurrent education must therefore avoid becoming a set of monolithic or restrictive institutions which continue to limit our response to change. On the contrary, a recurrent education strategy must envisage an institutional structure which is itself able to adapt, to learn and to change. By limiting its main focus to only one part of the lifespan, and so conditioning people to regard education as something finished and left behind with their youth, the present education system has rendered itself incapable of responding to the learning demands generated by rapid social change.

There is no coherence in the education provided after school and no serious awareness of the various adult problems generated by change. While the need for updating work skills has belatedly been recognized, the need for updating 'life skills' is still largely ignored. Training can take place at many times in life – education only once. Yet there is a continuing need throughout life for knowledge of all kinds; there is, in some cases, a need to 'unlearn'; there is a recurring need to learn about oneself as well as about one's society. Because it is predicated on change, because it would have a built-in capacity to respond to change, recurrent education can be seen as the last, as well as the most fundamental, structural reform in education. For, while the content and methods of learning would have to be consciously and continually altered to meet new conditions and needs, the institutions of recurrent education, and the attitudes of the people who run them, would ensure that these new learning needs were automatically incorporated in the existing structure and provision of education, with no disruption or unnecessary time lag. Once it has been enshrined in policy that, in addition to its role as repository of human knowledge and of civilized values, the education system must take on a complementary role of providing appropriately structured forms of learning for all individuals at recurring intervals throughout the length and breadth of life, the challenge of change holds fewer problems.

Enough has already been said about recurrent education to show that it is linked with social situations and educational dilemmas unique to the latter part of the twentieth century. It is no accident that international organizations have played a large part in formulating and developing the ideas associated with recurrent education, because the problems of education are truly world-wide. The shift in developing countries, in a very short period, from tribal social organization and hunting or agricultural economies to more individualistic organization and a much more industrial or urban economy, has highlighted the need to educate adults as well as children, for adults not only have to create the changes in these countries, they also have to survive the cultural shocks of rapid change. In Britain the problems may be more complicated, and attitudes and institutions more rigidly established, but the logic is the same. Children no longer create the future that counts; their turn will come the day after tomorrow. Tomorrow's world is being created and experienced by today's adults. In this simple formulation lies the novelty of recurrent education. Recurrent education is more than a new name. It is an educational response to a completely new situation in the human experience.

Nevertheless, one of the charges against recurrent education is that there is nothing new in it. To some extent this attack can be justified, but only by coming to the pleasing conclusion that recurrent education, its goals and its ideals, if not its detailed proposals, is in harmony with the thought of all the major educational thinkers of the past.

Recurrent education vehemently denies the equation, frequently called 'traditional', between education and schooling. This 'tradition', like many strongly cherished beliefs, is in fact firmly rooted in the nineteenth century. Taking a broader historical and global perspective, one can establish an extremely powerful cultural tradition which regards education as a natural habit throughout life, albeit in most cases only for privileged minorities. Recurrent education can draw moral strength from a tradition in which Aristotle felt the study of politics should be the province of mature adults only, and in which Socrates stands out supreme as a non-directive, extra-mural adult educator. His nearest challenger, perhaps, is Jesus of Nazareth, who, it seems, merely allowed the children to draw near on one occasion, instead of insisting on their presence each weekday at 9 a.m.

Confucius in China, Manu in India, the great philosophers in all cultures, at least up to the nineteenth century, recognized education as a seamless robe, even if, like Luther, they were especially concerned to instil good habits in childhood. We are told that the child going to a medieval school 'immediately entered the world of adults'.[12] Comenius appears especially modern in this respect despite his optimistic belief in the possibility of encyclopaedic learning in all branches of knowledge. His rationale for both mass and life-long education is cogent and persuasive. Given that life is lived for the greater glory of God, education must be the means of making it good enough for Him, and this is clearly a lifelong process. Moreover, since the whole of life in all its aspects is subservient to this higher good, education must concern itself with the daily routine of living as well as with loftier forms of mental activity. Hence lifelong and life-wide education must be aimed for. In the modern world recurrent education faces the task of implementing these 'vertical' and 'horizontal' approaches to education, without Comenius' dependence on transcendentalism.

Since the industrial revolution, education has become separated not just from God but from life itself, so that for most people it is merely a brief interlude before 'real' life begins. William Morris recognized this happening over ninety years ago. He castigated child-dominated education as a 'niggardly dole of not very accurate information . . . accompanied by twaddle which it was well known was of no use'.[13] Like Dewey after him he wanted education to concern itself with personal growth, and in his ideal society personal growth was a lifelong process shaped by each individual's aptitudes and disposition.

Although modern conceptions of recurrent education and associated ideas owe most to French writers – Jessup has traced the origins of *l'education permanente* to the desire of French resistance fighters to build a better world after the Second World War[14] – the rather older tradition of British adult education offers much material to refute those who would like to dismiss recurrent education as a passing gimmick. The pioneering ideas and work of Maurice, Mansbridge and Tawney are well known.[15] So too is the famous demand of the 1919 Report on Adult Education for 'universal lifelong adult education'.[16] Most inspiring of all early writing on the topic, however, is by a little-known member of the committee which produced the 1919 report, B. A. Yeaxlee. His book, called *Lifelong Education*, was published in 1929, and his stirring demand for universality and comprehensiveness in recurrent education is made even more urgent today by the challenge of change:

> Adult education must provide not only for the people who have had secondary and university education, or who would have profited if it had fallen to their lot, but also for those who, if the highroad had been flung open, neither would nor could have set foot upon it.[17]

References

1   A. Toffler, *Future Shock*, London, Bodley Head, 1970.

2 D. A. Schon, *Technology and Change – the New Heraclitus*, Oxford, Pergamon, 1967.

3 Department of Employment, *The Changing Structure of the Labour Force – A Project Report by the Unit for Manpower Studies*, London, HMSO, 1976.

4 Quoted in R. Jungk, *Brighter than a Thousand Suns*, Harmondsworth, Penguin, 1964, p. 19.

5 Buckminster Fuller, 'The Year 2000', *Architectural Design*, February 1967, p. 62.

6 H. Kahn and B. Bruce Briggs, *Things to Come*, New York, Macmillan, 1972.

7 A. C. Clarke, *Profiles of the Future*, London, Pan, 1964, p. 20.

8 Quoted in D. Bergamini, *Japan's Imperial Conspiracy*, London, Panther, 1972, p. 234.

9 R. Nisbet, *The Social Philosophers*, London, Paladin, 1976, p. 446.

10 P. F. Drucker, *The Age of Discontinuity*, London, Pan, 1971, pp. 15ff.

11 J. Bronowski, *The Ascent of Man*, London, BBC Publications, 1973, p. 437.

12 Robert of Salisbury, quoted in P. Aries, *Centuries of Childhood*, London, Jonathan Cape, 1962, p. 153.

13 W. Morris, *The Collected Works of William Morris*, Vol. XVI (News From Nowhere), London, Longman, Green and Company, 1912, pp. 63–4.

14 F. Jessup, 'L'education permanente', *Studies in Adult Education*, no. 5, April 1973, pp. 16–25.

15 F. D. Maurice, *Learning and Working*, W. E. Styler (ed.) Oxford University Press, 1968. A. Mansbridge, *An Adventure in Working Class Education: Being the Story of the Workers' Educational Association 1903–15*, London, Longman, 1920; R. H. Tawney, *The Radical Tradition*, R. Hinden (ed.), London, George Allen & Unwin, 1964.

16 *Final Report of the Adult Education Committee of the Ministry of Reconstruction*, Chairman A. L. Smith, London, HMSO, 1919.

17 B. A. Yeaxlee, *Lifelong Education*, London, Cassell, 1929, p. 153.

Chapter 3

Facing up to Change

The greatest problems of psychological adaptation and adjustment arise when people are forced to change whether they wish to or not, and it is the world of work which brings out these problems in their most intense form. This chapter looks at the difficulties which individuals and institutions have to face when economic or technological circumstances force them to change, and suggests how recurrent education might be able to ease the processes of transition for both individuals and the organizations in which they work.

For nearly everyone work is an important aspect of life. Not only do we spend a great deal of waking time carrying it out, but most of us tend to use the work that we do to support the personality structure which tells us who we are. Severe psychological problems arise from unemployment. George Orwell, in *The Road to Wigan Pier*, describes the shame of a working man at being unemployed, the shame of seeing his hands becoming softer and whiter than his wife's. There is the cry of a Polish worker: 'How hard and humiliating it is to bear the name of an unemployed man. When I go out I cast down my eyes because I feel wholly inferior.'[1] For men loss of work can be an emasculation, and the attitudes expressed to the removal of the opportunity to work show that work is more than just a habit or a means of gathering income. There is no evidence that unemployment is any more acceptable in Britain in the late 1970s than it was in the 1930s, or that there is any widespread abstention from the work ethic on which industrialized societies are based.

Those educationists who would like to deny the crucial role that people's occupations play in their lives should perhaps examine the importance of their own work to themselves.

Men are using their occupations as a definition of their usefulness, as a way of acquiring status and as a way, almost, of establishing their manhood. If one were to stop men in the street and ask 'Who are you?' they would quickly use their occupation to help them in their reply. Two American researchers produced a formalized technique and conducted a survey of this kind.[2] People were asked to make three answers to the question 'Who are you?' and the most common set of responses was name, sex and occupation. Across the whole of the survey 61 per cent mentioned occupation as one of their three replies. Moreover, this identification with occupation is not solely confined to older people who have been at work longer. Individuals establish a conception of themselves as members of an occupational group quite rapidly during their period of induction into work or during training. A similar pattern of development takes place with both professional and manual workers once they have begun their training, even though professionals tend to start their training when they are older.[3] It would seem that the assumption of an occupational role is a very important part of maturation. Piaget says that 'The focal point of the decentering process is the entrance into the occupational world or the beginning of serious professional training. The adolescent becomes an adult when he undertakes a real job.'[4] As Galinsky and Fast point out, 'In our society one of the most clearcut avenues through which identity concerns are expressed is the process of making a vocational choice. The vocational choice is often the first important decision with which one is faced that will have marked effects on later experience.'[5]

The taking-up of an occupational role helps the individual to begin to establish a mature social identity which becomes stable and strongly defined. But, as has already been pointed out, it is becoming increasingly necessary for people to be retrained into different fields of work. For the mature worker this can be an extremely difficult period of adjustment, because the retraining implies the loss of all the status and strengths gained by the investment of energy and time in developing their original skill or particular set of techniques. The identity structure which has been founded on this skill needs to be broken down during the process of retraining and a new role established.

Ralph Ruddock, in his essay in *Six Approaches to the Person*,[6] attempts to establish a model on the basis of which one can sort out the various roles which individuals play as part of their lives. He has produced the image of a 'role tree', in which the tree trunk is the primary role, e.g. a middle-aged man, the main branches are the general roles, e.g. husband, father, worker, and other secondary branches and twigs represent sub-roles which lie within these general roles. It could be suggested that for many individuals, as a result of the social environment, the growth of this tree has led to an over-development of the branches concerned with occupation. Just as a map of the nervous system exaggerates the size of the mouth and the dominant hand, so a map of the identity structure would exaggerate the importance of the occupational roles. There is no doubt that occupational roles have become dominant within the system and have tended to influence and to decrease the importance of other aspects. This imbalance exists, and wishful thinking by educationists will not remove it. It will not disappear purely because economic trends reduce the need for manpower and give rise to structural unemployment. There is a lag in perception which would lead people to search for and expect 'careers' when the concept is perhaps already becoming anachronistic. The way to resolve this imbalance, this disproportionate emphasis, is not to ignore occupation and concentrate on the areas of activity around and outside it. Rather, it is to accept that occupation will play a part in people's lives, and to attempt to absorb it into a whole pattern within which it plays a less dominant role. Survival against the background of change will require a versatility in role play, the ability to gain identity supports from the full range of roles in the role tree. It is necessary to prune back the occupational branches and encourage growth elsewhere. This can only be done within a recurrent education service which deals with people as whole beings and which does not fragment their needs.

The traditional view that education is concerned with the world outside work, and the more recent emphasis on education for leisure, both make the assumption that alienation is not only inevitable but also creative! It seems that the alienation which Marx saw as arising inevitably from the structure of industrial society has become embedded in the socialization process. The modern idea of liberal education presupposes that occupation is always sterile. Such a perspective devalues the activity which takes up much of our waking lives and happily accepts the fragmentation of the individual. A mass education system has to work within the framework of a mass preoccupation with work, however unpalatable this may be to the academic establishment. The difficulties of training mature workers certainly stem from feelings of alienation; but theirs is an alienation from education, not from work.

Most industries accept the need to help their workers to update skills and many successful retraining schemes operate, particularly where a worker remains in the same general skill area. The worst problems occur when men are attempting to make drastic changes in their type of work, e.g. miners moving above ground or railwaymen moving into factory work. These problems arise because there is nothing in our traditional modes of education and training which programmes men or women to be adaptable. What makes it so difficult to retrain?

R. M. and Eunice Belbin, the founders of the Industrial Training Research Unit, have gathered a great deal of experience in the problems which arise during the training of mature workers. In *Problems of Adult Retraining*, a series of case studies, they quote an instructor on the stress experienced by older men during training: 'Men change from being calm, at ease and relaxed, to being so tense you dare not go near them.'[7] It has been shown by physiological tests that training is a rather more stressful activity for older than for younger workers. In fact the stress and the threats to the established personality structure are so severe that many people do not accept retraining opportunities, or drop out once they have begun. Again, the Belbins quote a skilled man in the chemical industry who, offered retraining by his firm, failed to carry the course to its conclusion: 'I was just scared of not passing the second year exam or of falling behind the others. You see I've been a leading hand and I have a reputation to keep up.'[8] This worker was frightened of failure. This unwillingness to risk a loss of status established in a former occupation is often the cause of a great waste of individual potential. At the same time it contributes to a waste of national resources. At a time when over $1\frac{1}{4}$ million were unemployed in Britain, and when many firms were pointing to a shortage of skilled labour as a limiting factor on development,[9] 4,704 out of at total of 18,480 Skill-centre places were not taken up. This included 38 per cent of the places for electrical and electronic engineering, 31 per cent of those for engineering production and 24 per cent of those for instrumentation engineering.[10] Resistance to retraining at this level is both an individual and a national problem, and overcoming this resistance will be a key factor in both individual and national development.

If maximizing the opportunities for personal development is an aim of education, the work-place is an essential arena for educational activity. It is important to develop structures in which work and education at least collaborate, and at best are fused together, to avoid psychological stress in adulthood and to cultivate adaptability. The failure of many existing training schemes to help people adapt to change is directly related to their previous experience of formal learning at school. Where such experience has been positively unpleasant, or even merely irrelevant, there is a natural reluctance to repeat it. To quote the Belbins: 'The shunning of training and its counterpart, tenacious attachment to jobs that are familiar ... are often linked with a long separation from, and a distaste for, formal education.'[11] They suggest that any experience of education or training since leaving school appears to help with later adaptation to some types of learning. For most working people, however, education has been gratefully left at the first available opportunity.

The present mode of compulsory schooling applied to those aged between 5 and 16 – those, in other words, who are considered immature, not responsible for their own decisions and dependent upon adults for maintenance – has produced an attitude in people's minds which associates all formal learning with immaturity. Henry Morris saw this danger: 'We are so ridden by departmentalized views of education, so prone to look upon education as a parenthesis in the human adventure, that in thinking about education we think solely of the school.'[12] By implication, therefore, any further learning is seen as a regressive experience. By concentrating our education on children we have made learning an activity appropriate to childhood, and when we have become men we put away childish things. Willingness to learn is a prerequisite for adaptability. As a result of the present pattern and emphasis of education, there is little willingness to learn, and hence no encouragement to adaptability. A useful sidelight on this issue can be drawn from Maurice Punch's study of Dartington Hall School, *Progressive Retreat*.[13] His study shows the problems which can arise when an institution is out of phase with its background society – its surrounding environment. Dartington Hall School has been in the forefront of the progressive education movement since the 1930s, but Punch suggests that some students found that the values and attitudes expressed by the school were so different from those outside that they found it difficult to reconcile them. What had been conceived as an enabling institution in fact functioned as a disabling institution. These students found leaving the school a very great problem and had difficulty establishing regular working and living patterns. Punch suggests that this relates to Goffman's work on the inmates of total institutions: 'It is crucial to appreciate that difficulty in leaving is common in many expressive total institutions such as public schools, service academies and even Oxbridge colleges.'[14] The state secondary school could be examined in the same light. The values and attitudes expressed by the institution are similarly out of key with the real world, but the real world is within the student's everyday experience. The institution thus loses credibility, and the attitudes which underlie it are devalued. Once again the institution disables. But the state secondary school does not disable its students for work – far from it. Students would like to leap into jobs from the school gate. Their disablement is from education itself. They are disabled from any return to learning because the idea that learning is a valuable skill has been discredited by its context.

All the pressures of the present education system are opposed to any easy transfer between earning and learning. In fact our system of institutions could not be better designed to thwart such an approach. At the average school there is little to help the young person develop his conception of his occupational future before the fourth or fifth year, which are the tenth and eleventh years of his school career, and schools in general have a deep mistrust of the world of work. Rarely is the willingness to learn new skills and techniques stimulated in order to encourage adaptable behaviour in later life; it is only stimulated in order to achieve the short-term goals of the certification system. The patterns of behaviour and the content of the curriculum bear very little relation to the real world which young people know exists outside. For them the link between the school curriculum and this real world is perceived in terms

of the need to secure the right kinds of examination passes.
As a result the world outside the school gains an attractive-
ness which has no relation to the realities of work.

The raising of the school-leaving age has extended the lag
between the age at which people become physically mature
and the first point at which they can adopt and practise
roles appropriate to mature status. J. M. Tanner, an authority on adolescent development, makes the following
suggestion:

> Where society does not permit the adolescent to assume a
> social role compatible with his physical and intellectual
> development, but keeps him dependent and irresponsible at
> home, adult maturity is come by with more difficulty.[15]

It is the occupational role which is the first adult role for
many young people, and it is the opportunity to play this
role which is withheld.

The emphasis on schooling between the ages of 5 and 16
and the growing time lag between young people's physical
maturity and their assumption of mature roles lead to the
school-leaver preferring work to school because, by this
stage, the illusion is deeply rooted that it is a choice of freedom, maturity and independence over restriction, immaturity
and dependence. Frank Musgrove, in *Youth and the Social
Order*,[16] and in his observations on the raising of the school-
leaving age,[17] expressed a stronger version of this view; he
asserted that, functionally speaking, prolonged school and
college education of a kind which he called 'liberal' acts to
retard the maturation of the young. He certainly found that
grammar-school children tended to be more confused about
their relationship with adult models than secondary-modern
schoolchildren. He found that grammar-school children who
were subjected to prolonged liberal education, education
for its own sake, took their models from their peer group,
whereas the secondary-modern schoolchildren were gradually approaching maturity by following the adults around

them.[18] In this sense the prolonged liberal education was creating a separate youth culture.

Ironically, the results of existing education patterns can be as damaging to the 'successes' as to the 'failures'. For different reasons, both tend to become inflexible in later life, and less capable than they should be of facing up to the challenge of change. The 'failures', understandably, are reluctant to submit themselves to more education and new forms of learning, however necessary these may be for their successful adaptation to new conditions, because they associate learning with childhood, dependence and failure. The 'successes', on the other hand, having established early in life, as a result of educational achievement, what they regard as a stable occupational identity, are reluctant to let it go; and they, too, tend towards inflexibility in the face of new conditions requiring new approaches. Herman Kahn calls this 'educated incapacity', an 'acquired or learned inability to understand or see a problem'.[19] One result is that if a problem, or a solution to a problem, lies outside the known and accepted framework, it is often more difficult for the specialist to perceive than the amateur. The notion that extended liberal education early in life is the key to a flexible personality can no longer be taken on trust.

Charles Kadushin found a related problem when looking at the development of a professional identity among music students in New York: 'Administrators and teachers in both schools feel that too early a development of professional self-concept is harmful to the ability of the students to remain in the student role and meet its requirements.'[20] It seems as though professional training, as it takes place, can lead to the closing-down of the mental aperture which permits the entry of new ideas. Yet, at the same time, prolonged education without commitment to a profession may keep the aperture open wide but at the expense of a mature social identity. The dilemma exists only because learning and earning are so divorced from each other.

The conflict can also be seen in courses of liberal or

general studies which are attached to industrial training programmes in order to retain an educational presence and, it is hoped, 'to broaden' the total provision. Such hopes are seldom realized. Research carried out with professional and skilled manual trainees shows that once they have developed a clear picture of their occupational future their tolerance of study which does not directly relate to their chosen work begins to decrease.[21] Some skilled manual trainees even begin to discriminate against the theoretical background to their trade.[22] Again, in working-class jobs, as in middle-class professions, the aperture begins to narrow and a desire to accept new learning diminishes. There is some evidence that it may be trainees who are unhappy with their chosen jobs who remain interested in learning in general and who are the most receptive students to general studies' programmes.[23] There is a clear difference, to cite another example, among students on teacher-training courses, between those who intend to become teachers and those who are using the course as a means to a generalized higher education. Those who intend to become teachers stress the need for more vocationally orientated courses, whereas those who are not committed to teaching put their emphasis on the more general background studies.[24] If teachers themselves are conditioned to think of their occupation as being totally distinct from their earlier student role, it is not surprising that every other group in society should make the same assumption of a radical break between earning and learning.

The root of the problem of rejecting education early in life, whether it is a conscious or an unconscious rejection, lies in the suddenness of the transition from a 'general' education to work or training. In the move to what appears a higher-status activity, i.e. the adult activity of work, the apprentices or students are only too keen to cast off all the baggage associated with the lesser activity. The sudden transition into work is no less damaging in the long term than the sudden shock of becoming unemployed in mid-career, already described, or the sudden transition out of work and into retirement. The literature on retirement is full of cases in which the loss of work leads to an early death. It is recognized that the psychological shock of retirement can be avoided by ensuring a gradual transition out of work over a period of months or years. It seems an obvious suggestion that the transition should be equally gradual at the start of work as well.

Working life can be seen as a kind of institutionalization where activity is structured, routines established and relationships forged, so that deep personal satisfactions, even identity itself, become associated with the work-place and with work-mates. Leaving the 'institution' has similarities, therefore, with leaving other kinds of long-term institutions. Erving Goffman has studied in great detail the effects of institutionalization and the psychological adjustments which the long-term prisoner or hospital patient has to make, both on entering and leaving their institutions.[25] It is clear that the move out of such an environment must be gradual, through parole or short visits to the outside community, if problems are to be avoided. Retirement presents a parallel. American researchers have shown that people who phase their withdrawal from work by keeping on a part-time job tend to maintain a higher morale than those who make a complete break.[26] In Britain some enlightened firms are beginning to handle retirement in this way, by allowing workers gradually to decrease the number of hours worked and become more accustomed to structuring their own time. In one firm the employee stops working overtime two years before retirement and for the last six months of his working life he works only a four-day week. Moreover, such firms, in common with some enlightened prison and hospital administrators, are recognizing that leaving their institutions is made easier through the provision of education, i.e. by providing appropriate forms of learning about the new situations and challenges of the outside world.

A similarly gradual and educational introduction to new situations and challenges is not yet seen as necessary, except in the most superficial way, at the other end of working life – at the beginning. The effect of this omission is more subtle. There is no sudden shock, as with unemployment or retirement; rather, there is likely to be joy at escaping the confines of school. However, the delayed action, which is no less significant for being largely unperceived, occurs in later life when, as we have seen, people are all too often stranded in mid-career, or even earlier, without the motivation to grasp the supports which education can offer. The polarization and separation of work and education early in life prevents adaptability in later life. The only way to arrive at a balance where earning and learning, security and adaptability, are not incompatible, where adopting an earning role does not preclude or severely limit the possibility of adopting learning roles, is to ensure that the two exist in harmony from the earliest possible point. Our management of socialization must ensure a smooth series of transitions. It is necessary to ensure that neither mode becomes branded with the stigma of childhood. One can imagine the situation if only those below the age of 16 worked, and if the adult business of the world were learning. How eager children would be to escape from the childhood world of work! Recurrent education envisages an end to the sudden transition from education to work. Only a balanced lifelong approach, giving equal weight to the various aspects of the managed socialization process, including early exposure to work, and the establishment of institutions which combine education and training functions for all ages, can break down the divisions and smooth out the discontinuities which have been illustrated. A system based on this principle would offer opportunities for the learning and practice of roles across the whole spectrum of social activity.

From an economic point of view, this kind of lifelong process would produce a labour force prepared and able to accept change. It would be flexibly trained and open to innovation, yet at the same time be able to accept that personal development through academic or non-vocational courses was a real possibility. In order to achieve these twin goals the balanced sequence of this form of recurrent education system would have to start at the earliest possible point in the child's development. The groundwork would be established at an early stage and doors could never be irrevocably closed. This requires a basic revaluation of the role of education and its links with other areas of life. An education system will only be able to achieve this balance if it develops in a co-ordinated way, explicitly recognizing that providing life chances and providing quality of life are interconnected, and not separate, goals. A recurrent education system with this unified approach would help individuals cope with change and resolve the problems it brings them in any sphere of life. Such a recurrent education system would also offer the institutions and organizations in which individuals function an approach to change and a way of managing new situations. The key to institutional change, as to personal adaptation, is flexibility.

The implementation of recurrent education must have as a starting-point the recognition that flexibility is an integral characteristic of the educational system. At first sight flexibility may not seem an appropriate concept to apply to education. Education has been traditionally concerned, above all, with the permanent and unchanging truths and values of human experience. But education in the late twentieth century needs to concern itself equally with change, with adjustment and with survival, for institutions as well as individuals.

In a society which is being forced to cope with changes resulting from technological innovation and economic upheaval, the difficulty is to ensure that the transitions are smooth from one set of circumstances to the next. There can never be enough information for the precise forward planning which will take every detail into account. Schon has pointed out that this is the major problem with which large institutions are faced in new situations.[27] The traditional way in which governments and large agencies operate when faced with a new problem and a consequent need to change policy is extremely cumbersome. The centre requests the information on which to base policy decisions from the peripheral, grass-roots operatives in the regions. By the time the information has been processed at the centre, a decision taken and passed back down the line to the periphery, the problem has probably changed its shape. The proposed solution is all too often out of date before it has even been tried. In *1066 and All That* the problems that Gladstone had in dealing with Ireland are described: '[he] spent his declining years trying to guess the answer to the Irish Question; unfortunately, whenever he was getting warm, the Irish secretly changed the Question.'[28]

This is becoming the problem of modern government. Even in such a crucial area as population growth, forecasting is very much a hit-and-miss affair. In 1955 it was expected that the population of the United Kingdom would remain stable for the following ten years, but in fact it rose by 30 per cent. In 1965 it was expected that the rise would continue, but it did not, and as a result in 1970 there were 25 per cent more children than had been predicted in 1955 but 4 per cent less than had been predicted in 1965. All areas of the social services are affected by this kind of forecasting, but the education service shows the pressures particularly clearly. In 1970 there were 1.7 million more children of school age than had been predicted in 1955, but in the late 1970s numbers were declining. From 1969 to 1976 the numbers entering primary schools had dropped by 90,000, and from 1977 to 1981 the number will fall to 290,000 below the 1969 level. There is a cycle of peaks and troughs in the numbers' graph as children pass through the system, with numbers declining in secondary schools from 1981 into the 1990s. At the same time, higher and further education, having increased their student numbers until the early 1980s, will then begin to contract. These national patterns will be modified by local conditions and by migration within Britain and immigration from without. There are therefore bound to be differing assessments of our future educational requirements, and they will appear quickly on one another's heels. The difference in school-building costs alone, between the 'low' projection and the 'central' projection, would be £700 million by 1995–6.[29]

What we know for certain is that our population is ageing. Between 1966 and 1976 the number of people aged 65 and over increased by 20 per cent, and by 1986 there will be 24 per cent more people aged 75 and over than there were in 1978.[30] With the additional possibility that early retirement may increase, to alleviate the unemployment situation, we can foresee tremendous problems of adaptation. To the demands which arise from shifts in the pattern of population, we must add the demands on education and training resulting from the other kinds of change already outlined.

All these difficulties and uncertainties come together in manpower planning. The ideal manpower plan would of course consist of a perfect match of the supply of labour, both in quantity and type, with the demand expected from employers. Unfortunately, both sides of this equation are, as we have noted, extremely resistant to reliable forecasting. Yet government must devise policies which will cope with these uncertainties, and their best instrument for successful intervention will be the country's education and training system. At present all these pressures have to be absorbed, and solutions found, in an educational system of considerable inflexibility, in which it takes, for example, four years to train a teacher and several years to design and build a school. One way *not* to cope with such pressures is to arrive at a position in which the only solution appears to lie in the wholesale closure, or piecemeal conversion, of valuable educational organizations like teacher-training colleges. This kind of solution is all too likely to turn out to be an example of the cumbersome decision-making process described above. By the time the colleges have been 'finally' closed, the situation will have changed and this particular 'solution' will have no relevance to the new problems.

It is necessary to develop some kind of planning and control which can smooth out the discontinuities and enable institutions to deploy personnel, plant and finance to the best advantage in changing situations. This is what is meant by 'institutional flexibility', and it is based on the assumption that changing functions is the norm, not just in an individual's working life, but also in the life of an institution or organization. This perspective requires that government should not only be able to fund new or increased demands but also recover the use of resources from agencies and institutions when pressures are reduced. If resources are allocated to cope with an upward swing in needs, they should also be freed when a downward swing takes place. The freedom to reallocate resources either within or between projects is crucial to the development of a flexible system with a reasonably short reaction time.

The Central Policy Review Staff (the 'Think Tank') have investigated this problem in relation to the most recent population bulge, and concluded that 'Rising numbers generate demands for proportionately more expenditure; static (or relatively declining) numbers do not yield proportional savings. This asymmetry is suspect.'[81] Agencies which have been given greater resources to sustain them through crisis can absorb the increased funds when the demands are reduced. This is typical of what Donald Schon has called 'dynamic conservatism' – the tendency of an institution to fight to retain its shape and status even when it becomes 'a memorial to past problems'. Schon uses the example of the US agricultural extension service, which was established to improve farming methods during the era of the dust-bowl and depression, but which grew and continued to grow when agricultural surpluses were being burnt and poured down coal-mines.[82] The maternity service in Britain is an example that the 'Think Tank' quotes. Despite the recent decline in the birth rate there has been little decline in expenditure on the maternity services – more women have babies in hospital.[83] This institutional inflexibility is clearly linked to the individual inflexibility which we described earlier in the chapter. Individuals who have invested time and status in a certain type of training, to carry out work within a certain kind of institution, do not easily accept the notion of continual change in their working lives. It would seem unreasonable in the present contexts of work and career expectations to say to a midwife or gynaecologist that 'There is no longer any need for you – retrain as something else'! They could with justice point to the projected demand for an expansion of the maternity services at the end of the 1980s to cope with the expected births from the girls born in the bulge of the early 1960s. As the 'Think Tank' pointed out:

> There is no reason to expect that in the foreseeable future governments will be able to finance the rate of increase in social services as, say, in the recent past, certainly not to exceed them, and public expectations will need to accommodate this. But needs will change and priorities with them. Resources will have to be provided in part by switching from one programme to another. The room for such switching will be affected, to an important extent, by the responsiveness of the programme to demographic change.[34]

But responsiveness to demographic change, although important, is not enough. It is never enough just to respond to change. The people involved in implementing the new programmes, the organizations for which they work, and the policy-makers who make the switches from one programme to another, will all need to have been pre-adapted to expect these changes.

This means that in all areas of work the fundamental human and psychological need for security will have to be separated from the strong historical and social expectations of stability and continuity in life and career patterns. Psychological security can be achieved in periods of flux if people are prepared for the unknown in constructive ways, and if organizations recognize the need for their members to feel secure. Recurrent education, in one sense, is the means of providing a foreground of a secure identity against an inevitable background of instability and discontinuity. Work, change and education become an interacting triad of concepts which have their effect throughout adult life and lead to the development of strong, stable identities which are based on this interaction rather than on any specific occupation. This is the meaning of 'individual flexibility'. At present people in training institutions tend to narrow the focus of the lens which lets through ideas and information and they exclude things which are not directly relevant to their specific vocational need. Having produced inflexible people, through educational institutions which are themselves inflexible, it should be no surprise that society ends up with inflexible institutions in all its spheres. This is a restatement of our paradox – that the development of an occupational identity through contact with work and training plays a large part in the development of a mature and stable identity, but the development of too rigid an occupational or professional self-concept is the root of inflexibility.

In this circular dilemma flexibility must become a key concept in policy. Ways must be found to make institutions flexible so that they can help people to be flexible. Gregory Bateson considers it an important enough concept to make it the base of a definition of a 'healthy ecology of human civilization'. He suggests that such a healthy ecology would be characterized by 'a single system of environment combined with high human civilization in which the flexibility of the civilization shall match that of the environment to create an ongoing complex system, open-ended for slow change of even basic . . . characteristics'.[85] In other words, a healthy civilization would be able to cope creatively with any changes in the background against which it functions. In such a civilization even the most fundamental attitudes and patterns of life would have a built-in capacity for change. A civilization like this would be pre-adapted for change; its cultural, social and economic agencies would expect change as a normal function. A recurrent system of education is one way of creating a society in which people can adapt without trauma, and function in institutions that can live with change without upheaval.

There are institutions already displaying flexible approaches, as Donald Schon pointed out in *Beyond the Stable State*.[36] Schon considered his theme to be institutions as learning systems, and this notion is central to any recurrent system of education. His work suggests that the seeds of the kind of flexible, responsive institutions which we are advocating for education can be found amongst the large multinational companies who have had to live with changes in the economic environment for many years. There are survival mechanisms that such industrial undertakings have developed which could be carried into general institutional practice. What Schon calls 'raising the level of aggregation'[37] is a good example. This is a practical way of making sure that the firm is not taken by surprise, that it has built-in expectations of change. A simple example would be the firm which, having traditionally made nails, broadens its fields of vision and prospective markets by thinking about fasteners in general and all methods of joining things together. By developing this broader strategy the firm pre-adapts for change within its industry, and by widening its research it can also influence the direction of that change. The liberating effect of this attitude can be seen in another case of a designer who, instead of thinking about designing chairs, thinks about the general problem of supporting bodies. He may come up with a bag stuffed with polystyrene which can serve the same purpose. An analogy might be the athlete better balanced to move in any direction because his feet are wide apart. He has a more generally useful base from which to move.

It is this idea of raising the level of aggregation, of increasing the generality of an institution, which the 'Think Tank' suggest as a strategy for the maternity service. Their problem was to discover the optimum level of aggregation for the hospital service as a whole, and hence the right way of allocating resources for maternity work. The 'Think Tank' proposal was that maternity work, rather than being housed in single-purpose units, should be a part of general hospitals at district level, so that wards can be converted to accommodate short-term increases in numbers of births and then converted back if necessary:

> An important means of ensuring greater flexibility is to reduce the number of single-purpose maternity units outside district general hospitals . . . Maternity provision within district general hospitals gives greater scope for the redeployment of beds and other resources.[38]

This recommendation goes against the current direction of development, which is towards single-purpose units. But flexible use of resources requires just this development of changeable plant and personnel. For the maternity service this would entail the movement of obstetricians to gynaecology during periods of low birth rate and the use of GPs to supplement specialist obstetricians at times of high birth rate. An essential corollary of raising the level of aggregation is the provision within organizations for a more generalized training of staff.

Establishing the optimum level of aggregation for any organization is clearly crucial. What is the right size for an organization which will enable it to reapportion budgets and restructure itself? How broad and generalized can its objectives be? In the educational world the level of aggregation has been set at the comprehensive school. The school's perspective covers a range of educational options for 11- to 18-year-olds, and ideally the switching of resources is facilitated. But a comparable recurrent education institution would have as its perspective the fullest possible range of structured learning experiences over the whole lifetime.

Another useful model for a flexible educational institution is what Schon calls the 'constellation firm'.[39] This is an idea drawn from the operating pattern of multinational conglomerates. The heart of the firm is a holding company, which is the repository of financial and management expertise. This central core starts and closes subsidiary firms to follow trends in demand. The winding-up of a subsidiary as needs change does not compromise the reputation or standing of the whole. In an educational context the central core would be the management, the body controlling the resources, and its subsidiaries might be the courses, or groups of courses, which it generates to meet needs. As in industry, the waxing and waning of these subsidiaries would not compromise the success of the whole institution. Once again the professional staff operating in such a fashion would need a generalized training.

Before looking in more detail at the implications of these two models for a recurrent system of education in Britain, we must look at the existing system to see where flexibility is most needed and where there might be a possible redeployment of resources if the principle of recurrence and the lifelong perspective were to be accepted.

References

1 B. Zanadski and P. Lazarsfeld, 'The Psychological Consequences of Unemployment', *Journal of Social Psychology*, 1935, pp. 224–51.

2 J. F. T. Bugental and S. L. Zelen, 'An Investigation into the Self-concept', *Journal of Personality*, vol. 18, 1950, pp. 483–98.

3 R. A. Flude, 'Occupational Self-concept and Commitment to a Trade among Groups of Printing Apprentices', unpublished MEd thesis, University of Birmingham, 1975.

4 B. Inhelder and J. Piaget, *The Growth of Logical Thinking from Childhood to Adolescence*, London, Routledge & Kegan Paul, 1958, p. 346.

5 M. D. Galinsky and J. Fast, 'Vocational Choice as a Focus of the Identity Search', *Journal of Counselling Psychology*, vol. 13, no. 1, 1966, pp. 89–92.

6 R. Ruddock, *Six Approaches to the Person*, London, Routledge & Kegan Paul, 1972, pp. 105–8.

7 R. M. Belbin and Eunice Belbin, *Problems in Adult Retraining*, London, Heinemann, 1972, p. 163.

8 Ibid, p. 168.

9 Confederation of British Industry, *Trends in Industry*, April 1978.

10 Account of information supplied to Frank Hooley, MP, by Department of Employment, in the *Guardian*, 30 May 1978, p. 2.

11 Belbin and Belbin, *Problems in Adult Retraining*, p. 36 (see note 7 above).

12 H. Morris, 'The New Senior School in Britain', a broadcast by the North American Service of the BBC, 14 September 1942, quoted in H. Rée, *Educator Extraordinary: The Life and Achievement of Henry Morris 1889–1961*, London, Longman, 1973, p. 81.

13 M. Punch, *Progressive Retreat*, Cambridge University Press, 1977.

14 Ibid, p. 101.

15 J. M. Tanner, *Growth at Adolescence*, Oxford, Blackwell, 1962, p. 218.

16 F. Musgrove, *Youth and the Social Order*, London, Routledge & Kegan Paul, 1964.

17 F. Musgrove, 'Childhood and Adolescence', in Schools Council Working Paper No. 12, *The Educational Implications of Social and Economic Change,* London, 1967, p. 58.

18 Musgrove, *Youth and the Social Order*, ch. 5 (see note 16 above).

19 Kahn and Bruce Briggs, *Things to Come*, p. 80 (see note 6 to Chapter 2).

20 C. Kadushin, 'The Professional Self-concept of Music Students', *American Journal of Sociology*, vol. V, 1969–70, pp. 389–404.

21 R. A. Flude, 'The Development of an Occupational Self-concept and Commitment to an Occupation in a Group of Skilled Manual Workers', *Sociological Review*, vol. 25, no. 1, February 1977, pp. 41–50.

22 Flude, 'Occupational Self-concept and Commitment to a Trade among Groups of Printing Apprentices' (see note 3 above).

23 Flude and M. T. Whiteside, 'Occupational Identity, Commitment to a Trade and Attitudes to Non-vocational courses amongst a Group of Craft Apprentices', *Vocational Aspect of Education*, vol. XXIII, no. 55, Summer 1971, pp. 69–72.

24 A. Smithers and S. Carlisle, 'Reluctant Teachers', *New Society*, 5 March 1970.

25 E. Goffman, *Asylums*, Harmondsworth, Penguin, 1968.

26 B. Kutner, D. Fanshel, A. Togo and T. S. Langner, 'Factors related to Adjustment in Old Age', in R. G. Kuhlen and G. G. Thompson (eds), *Psychological Studies of Human Development*, 3rd ed., New York, Appleton Century Croft, 1970, p. 583.

27 D. A. Schon, *Reith Lectures*, 1970, printed in the *Listener*, vol. 84, no. 2173–8. An extended treatment of the theme is to be found in D. A. Schon, *Beyond the Stable State: Public and Private Learning in a Changing Society*, London, M. T. Smith, 1971.

28 W. E. Sellers and R. J. Yeatman, *1066 and All That*, Harmondsworth, Penguin, 1960, p. 116.

29 *Population and the Social Services*, Report by the Central Policy Review Staff, London, HMSO, 1977.

30 *A Happier Old Age*, Department of Health and Social Security, Discussion Document, London, HMSO, 1978, p. 7.

31 *Population and the Social Services*, p. 52 (see note 29 above).

32 Schon, *Reith Lecture No. 5* (see note 27 above).

33 *Population and the Social Services*, p. 15, para. 6.3 (see note 29 above).

34 Ibid, p. 59, para. 17.2.

35 G. Bateson, 'Ecology and Flexibility in Urban Civilization', in *Steps to an Ecology of Mind*, London, Paladin, 1973, p. 470.

36 Schon, *Beyond the Stable State* (see note 27 above).

37 Schon, *Reith Lecture No. 3*. See *Beyond the Stable State*, chs 3–4 (see note 27 above).

38 *Population and the Social Services*, p. 16, para. 6.6 (see
    note 29 above).
39 Schon, *Reith Lecture No. 3*. See *Beyond the Stable State*,
    chs 3–4 (see note 27 above).

Chapter 4

The Lifelong Perspective

The previous chapters have outlined the meaning and significance of recurrent education in the conditions of late twentieth-century Britain. The premise is that the process of socialization can no longer be regarded as a once-and-for-all event. A recurrent education system would provide the means by which a society could manage the lifelong process of socialization of the individuals in it. But socialization is not just a passive phenomenon; it is simultaneously an active process of personal development. The recurrent education we envisage is in some ways a typically British compromise, hard-headed in that it denies the necessity for widespread reorganization of the social structure, yet radical in that it assumes social change and individual development to be both inevitable and desirable. In our view, recurrent education provides both theoretical and practical structures to suggest that it is not impossible, at least in the context of existing democratic values, to create an education system which can serve individual members of society and their social organizations at the same time. This optimistic view of the potential of recurrent education is tested in the next two chapters by an examination of the existing education and training system, which fails to serve either satisfactorily. At present the process of socialization is truncated and fragmented. Recurrent education implies developmental opportunities throughout the life span and over a broad range of life activity. This chapter points out some areas where the provision of these lifelong options is hampered in the existing British system.

These criticisms of existing education run counter to the official British view, publicly expressed at the European Ministers of Education Conference in 1975 in Stockholm, that recurrent education has little to do with existing educational provision, that it means additions to, rather than reorganization of, the present forms of education. Sooner rather than later this official view of recurrent education will have to change, if the concept is to be taken seriously. The seeming choice in strategies, between, on the one hand, attaching a system of 'recurrent education' on to the end of the existing 'front-end' system, and, on the other, redeploying resources from the present child-centred system to finance opportunities throughout life, is falsely presented. There is no real choice at all. The former may appear more acceptable politically at present, since it would merely require the assembly of some structure out of the building bricks of existing post-school institutions, but it would not work. A system of recurrent education which started after schooling had finished would be impossibly expensive. It is obvious that even with the temporary advantages of North Sea oil revenue Britain could not afford to provide comprehensive post-school education on the same scale as is presently provided for children. Anything less, however, would perpetuate the present attitude that schooling has top priority and everything else is less important.

Just as important as the financial impossibility of attaching recurrent education on to the end of schooling is the educational impossibility. Even if money were found to create extensive opportunities for the education and training of adults, a system which ignored schooling would be self-defeating. The will to use these opportunities simply would not exist. Early experiences of education largely determine whether later opportunities are taken up or not. In every form of European adult education at present, from paid educational leave, statutorily provided, to leisure-time evening activities, it is the better-educated minority, the 'successes' of the school systems, who predominate.[1] A system of recurrent education which does not affect the secondary school will merely continue the inequalities existing in the education system. Merely to extend the range of opportunities later in life will only succeed in providing more possible routes for those who are the educational 'haves'. It has been suggested that the surplus capacity which might become available in higher education in the 1990s could be used both to increase participation in higher education by working-class youngsters and to extend provision for the continuing education of potential adult students already in employment.[2] This desire for social justice, while wholly admirable in intention, would require massive positive discrimination to achieve even the appearance of success. Justice and equal opportunity in higher education can only spring from the creation early in life of the right attitude to learning. Social justice cannot emerge from an educational system that is based on competition and hierarchy from the age of 11. Most people simply do not look for more education after school. In a scheme of recurrent education the idea of leaving education behind with one's schooldays is anathema; yet in Britain today many pupils, perhaps the majority, leave having had, in their belief, not just enough education but enough *of* education. 'Developed' countries, such as Britain, need to take the same advice which they so freely offer to Third World countries:

> Little purpose can be served by attempts to graft new systems of adult education on to existing systems of schooling. This can result only in an unhappy articulation. New systems of adult education however make possible a comprehensive recasting of the whole process of schooling to the benefit of all age groups in the community and thence to the overall development process of the nation.[3]

If recurrent education is to mean anything, therefore, it

must affect present forms of education and it must lead to some redeployment of resources. Recurrent education is an alternative, not an addition, to the British system of education. Nevertheless, we believe that it can be introduced gradually, that there is no need for an upheaval in the 1980s and 1990s quite as great as comprehensive reorganization in the 1960s and 1970s. The mood in which this book is written is optimistic. It is necessary to point out the 'bad practices' in the mainstream of British education to throw into relief the 'good practices' which exist on the fringes, and which can ease the transition to recurrent education. The sooner changes start to be made, the less severe will disruptions have to be at a later stage. The rest of this chapter attempts to show where resources in education in general, and in secondary schools in particular, are not well used, and could therefore be made available for redeployment so as to create an effective recurrent education system.

Any redeployment of resources must start with the compulsory sector, since this is most people's only experience of education and since it consumes the bulk of the education budget. Within the compulsory sector it is the secondary school which provides the most fuel for criticism. Many criticisms are made of British primary and nursery education. On the whole, however, they reflect disagreement about methods rather than objectives. Despite the rhetoric of the Black Paper authors, most 'progressive' teachers at primary schools have been just as concerned as 'traditional' teachers to help their pupils achieve basic literacy and numeracy skills. Even the most 'formal' teacher must now be as convinced as his 'informal' counterpart of the importance of creative play and of self-expression in the development of young children from the earliest possible moment.

Secondary schools provide more fundamental causes for concern and disagreement, about objectives as well as methods. All institutions of education have developed their aims and policies in response to a range of varied demands over a long period of time. But the secondary school has had

5

the most expectations placed upon it and is creaking under the strain. Its objectives are both numerous and unstated, and they are becoming incompatible with one another. A brief list will show the pressure placed on secondary education by these diffuse aims. Secondary schools try to provide a good general education for all their pupils, most of whom will get no other. They attempt to give many pupils basic skills of a practical kind. They prepare some pupils for specialized courses in higher education. This preparation for a minority is achieved through the operation of a programme of examinations taken by nearly all their pupils. Hence these examinations have a dual role. They not only prepare pupils for higher or further education but also attempt to grade the pool of labour for potential employers. On top of these aims, secondary schools are taking on social support roles, and since attendance is compulsory they have been forced to become custodians and controllers of their pupils as well.

As if these aims and functions were not varied enough, to such a list must be added the egalitarian objectives of comprehensive school reformers, the idea of political education for democratic citizenship, the expectation that schools will provide a moral education, and recent concerns for the 'gifted child'. Given all this burden of expectations, the failings of secondary schools are in no way mysterious. The problem is one of overloading. Secondary education attempts to do too much in too short a time with pupils who are not necessarily at their most receptive. These problems can only grow worse as long as the attitude persists that an individual's life chances are entirely created in childhood, that education both equates and finishes with schooling. In a recurrent education system the objectives of secondary education would be limited. The general psychological framework would emphasize the similarity of adolescence and adulthood as contiguous and continuous periods of development. The specific task would be to prepare for the next stage, not for the whole of life. In recurrent education terms, adolescence is only one phase of development, and not necessarily the most important phase, in a lifetime. Each pupil would be launched into work, or initial training, or immediately continuing education, as well equipped as possible to cope with his or her present needs, and as well convinced as possible of their probable return to learning at later stages of life.

One effect of a recurrent education system would therefore be the taking of pressure off the secondary school. By limiting educational objectives to those which are most appropriately attained at that stage it would be possible to focus teaching effort on the development of individual children. Teachers would be major beneficiaries of recurrent education reforms, because many of the existing aims of secondary schools force them to adopt inappropriate methods. The situation is worse now than when Henry Morris wrote about the problem:

> Only after a ubiquitous and fully articulated system of adult education has been established can we afford to reform the curriculum followed by children, for only then would we be justified in persuading teachers to abandon their fallacy [the pedagogic fallacy, i.e. the use of texts and material too sophisticated for the age group in school], having the assurance that time and opportunity was available at a more appropriate moment in their lives for those things which are desirable but for which few children are ready.[4]

Although secondary schools are not identical, one common factor is their concern with external public examinations. The involvement of children in these examinations consumes vast resources of time, manpower and building space, as well as finance. Examinations deserve close scrutiny, therefore, when considering redeployment of educational resources, for the time and money spent on them might be better used to develop a recurrent education system. Many other aspects of secondary education might be criticized or considered as wasteful. But in our view it is the attitudes and values engendered by public examinations, and the image of education which this adolescent, academic steeplechase provokes in parents, teachers and pupils, which represent the main barrier to the development of recurrent education. Examinations have created the belief in education at school as the sole determinant of life chances, summed up in the evocative phrase, 'sacrificing the future of our children'.

As tools of education examinations have one set of functions. As tools of employers they have other, quite separate, functions. The compatibility of these functions, as well as their effectiveness, must be called into question. Successes in national examinations have become the main yardstick by which secondary schools prove to parents, pupils and public authorities that they are doing their job. Yet there is a strong case to be made that school examinations inhibit really effective education, are not good predictors of future educational successes and are not the best indication of job suitability. A sophisticated form of secondary education would look at these aspects separately for each child, rather than assume that a public examination system can meet such different requirements effectively and equitably.

Educationally, examinations may be used to assess and diagnose specific strengths or weaknesses, to predict future performance, or to measure attainment. These three uses must be looked at one at a time. Assessment and diagnosis play a crucial role in the curriculum development system. Assessment as a diagnostic exercise is partly a way of finding out how well teachers have followed and developed their teaching strategies; it is also a way to define the next set of objectives for each of the students. These objectives might be remedial, a consolidation or a development of learning. Yet public examinations, which take up most of the time and effort of pupils and teachers in secondary schools, have virtually no role as diagnostic agents for the individual learner, and have a negative effect on teaching strategy. It is left to other, internal forms of assessment, where there is time to implement them, to be used as guides to future individual learning requirements and to future teaching strategies. Some schools even find it necessary to devise internal assessment in order to decide which external examination is appropriate for particular children.

Public examinations are, however, used as predictors of future performance. They determine the entry of students to the world of higher education. But there is evidence that A levels are not good predictors of success at degree level.[5] In an appendix to the Robbins Report on Higher Education it was stated that 'Academic examinations are widely accepted as predictors [of university success] but are in fact not very good ones.'[6] Generally, researchers have found that the correlations between A-level performance and university examination results are low, but the difficulty of carrying out this kind of research is that those who do not get selected for university are not able to demonstrate their academic attainment. No realistic comparisons can therefore be made. In recent years, however, the Open University has shown that it is possible to carry out degree-level work successfully with students who have limited formal qualifications. In 1971, 6.3 per cent of those registering for Open University courses had no formal qualifications at all, and around 27 per cent had qualifications below those normally required for university entrance. In 1977, 7.8 per cent had no formal qualifications and over 35 per cent had less than the equivalent of two A levels.[7] Increasingly, success in Open University courses is being accepted as a qualification route in itself, as other conventional universities allow to successful OU students exemptions from parts of their degree courses.[8]

We are left with considerable doubts on the value of public examinations as anything more than the simple measurement of attainment on school courses. It would be useful if the public examination system could be shown to provide a nationally comparable measure of attainment in any particular subject. This would at least provide a fair basis for selection; but, in fact, there are considerable variations in the same subject between pupils' performances in different parts of the country,[9] and there are also considerable variations between the content of the syllabuses of different examination boards in the same subject.[10]

Even so, all criticism of public examinations would be greatly weakened if it could be shown that what pupils were expected to learn in the courses on which they are examined was an essential part of their development to adulthood, their path to a fuller and more satisfying life. If such were the case, it would hardly matter what use outside agencies made of the examination results: an education would have been provided in good faith for all children. But no teacher would agree that examination syllabuses provide a good general education for all children. The education which is measured by the present examination industry is a one-sided and overwhelmingly cognitive form of education. Examinations are based on the ability to recall knowledge, just as they were in 1934, when Ziliacus wrote of 'the child regarded as a gradually increasing fraction of a professor in each branch of study, doomed to swallow with or without cramming and at stated times to regurgitate for inspection those logically perfect but psychologically indigestible gobbets of erudition'.[11]

Nowadays one hears of a history teacher who wants only single periods with his A-level group, because 'they can't take notes for two whole periods'. The mere transfer and recall of knowledge is the lowest objective in Bloom's taxonomy, but this seems to make up the bulk of what can be measured in public examinations.[12] Some critics attack the way knowledge has been divided into traditional subject areas, but it is not the traditional subjects which are to blame. History, English Literature, Physics, Mathematics, Foreign Languages, etc., are ideal vehicles for developing the higher-order objectives of application, analysis, synthesis and evaluation. But teachers, even if they are eager to follow these roads to pupils' self-development, are hamstrung by the demands of the examination syllabus.

The Cognitive Research Trust has recently introduced

examinations in 'Thinking' in an attempt to counteract this tendency. Edward de Bono has described the need for such tests. He has characterized the school curriculum as being based on the sorting of available information and the search for more information. He distinguishes between 'input effectiveness', which implies the effective taking-in and absorption of knowledge, and 'output effectiveness', which implies an effectiveness in using knowledge that has already been absorbed or is readily available. 'In normal school circumstances,' he points out, 'it is very difficult to distinguish between the two . . . because the emphasis is so strongly on input effectiveness that a pupil who has failed to take in the required knowledge has no way of demonstrating any output effectiveness. If the input filter is blocked you are unlikely to get anything from the output of the pump.'[13] When education is seen merely as the transfer of knowledge it becomes, as Ilich suggests, a commodity rather than an activity.[14]

The syllabus in secondary schools is, after the age of 13 at least, almost entirely determined by examinations. The problem has long been recognized. In 1917 the Board of Education Circular 1002 stated that 'It is a cardinal principle that the examination should follow the curriculum not determine it.'[15] In 1943 the Norwood Committee criticized the way examinations were dominating the school curriculum.[16] Yet the tail of assessment continues to wag the dog of education, and we continue to devise examinable courses as if they were educational solutions. However well-intentioned the proposals for CEE, GCSE, N and F, or new written examinations in Industrial Studies, such innovations cannot help but become absorbed, just as CSE and General Studies became absorbed, in an examination-dominated setting in which any education measured and absorbed is perceived as subsidiary to the uses made of the assessment at the end of the course. It is these uses which cause concern. The examination industry has created a confusion between two concepts, each of which is on its own very important. Firstly, what does the individual need to know in order to take successfully a specific higher education course or to take up a specific occupation? Secondly, how do we decide, if the demand for places or jobs exceeds the supply, who should take the higher education course or who should get the job?

In some ways the educational limitations of public examinations, the fact that they do not measure very much that is worth measuring, and that they do not predict accurately future academic performance, are much less damaging than the inappropriate uses to which they are put by non-educational agencies. Examinations may not be very good *exact* predictors of success at university, but by and large intelligent pupils will become intelligent students. De Bono talks about the 'archway' effect, which states that 'if a stream of brilliant people go towards an archway, then from that archway will emerge a stream of brilliant people even if the archway has done no more than straddle their passage'.[17] Such an archway is merely an expensive irrelevance when it eases intelligent pupils into higher education. It does positive harm, however, and is a source of disenchantment with both education and work, when it leads to a glut of people who feel themselves 'over-qualified' for the jobs available to them.

It is the use made of public examinations, to select people for jobs and to sift out potential employees at all levels, which is their biggest fault, for they were never designed for that set of tasks. Job selection can and should be done by other means. Ivar Berg has pointed to the considerable problems faced by American employers as a result of recruitment through educational achievement. With regard to the armed forces, he suggests that 'there is scarcely a single programme . . . for which discrete measures of aptitudes, weak as they may be, are not much better predictors of performance than educational achievement'.[18] Employers believe that educational success in examinations shows potential for 'promotability', but Berg's case studies show that educational differences were less important in promotion than loyalty and long service. Analysis of US Department of Labor data shows that a growing number of people take up jobs which they feel are unworthy in view of their achievements in education. Job dissatisfaction is built in at the start of many people's working lives.[19]

Ronald Dore, whose book *The Diploma Disease* examines the place and purpose of examinations in several countries, including Britain, writes about the 'qualifications spiral' – the inflation in qualifications required for jobs. He quotes the case of librarianship in Britain, for which the School Certificate was a minimum requirement in 1950. By 1970 two A levels were required and in 1975 the Library Association was considering graduate entry only.[20] As these entry qualifications increase, so periods of apprenticeship, of *learning* the job, have been waived. Yet the content of the education which has been examined at O level, at A level, at degree level, and even at postgraduate level, may have only a minimal relationship with the work in the job. This is true at all levels of education and for all kinds of jobs or professions. Ironically, however, both school pupils and their parents, and many students in higher education as well, view examinations primarily as qualifications for work. The intrinsic educational merits of their courses are regarded as much less important.

The Schools Council Enquiry No. 1 showed strikingly the way that children and parents consider the instrumental role of the school to be the most important. Boys and girls aged 15 considered 'Teach you things which will help you to get as good a job as possible' as the most important role of the school.[21] Parents considered this the second most important role for boys, while head teachers rated it almost the least important. Frank Musgrove, in his *Preliminary Studies of a Technological University*, found that 'students of both social and physical sciences attached more importance than their teachers to the vocational relevance of their studies.'[22] From a recurrent education viewpoint it is interesting to note that 19 and 20-year-olds questioned as part of the Schools

Council Enquiry No. 1 were less concerned than the 15 and 16-year-olds with the direct vocational relevance of school work, since they felt that when they were at school they did not have sufficient knowledge of their own capabilities, or the possible jobs which might be available, to make sensible decisions about vocational courses. Education keeps young people away from the real world for longer and longer periods of time, to take examinations which have little value in educational terms, even less value in terms of later work experience, yet are believed by all to be essential to future success in life.

Within the existing framework it is not surprising that examinations are used by the professions in Britain to create a form of restrictive practice. In an age when more and more people are spending longer and longer in full-time education, the professions, if they are to maintain status and keep attracting the ablest young people, have no choice but to increase the level of qualifications required for entry. However, the professions are as guilty as anybody of perpetuating the weaknesses of the examination industry and preventing even minor reforms. By a system of 'exemptions for membership' they ensure that many students continue to take the narrowest possible path through higher education, even when some institutions of higher education are willing to offer a wide range of educational options through modular courses. As suggested in Chapter 3, a narrowness in the professionals' own early educational experience leads them to display this kind of inflexibility in later life, when their professions are faced with the problems of change. It is brave but futile for a Chief Education Officer to suggest that intelligent pupils should miss out A-levels and university by leaving school at 16 and serving an apprenticeship in industry. Only if a system of recurrent education had already been created would this be a feasible option, and a system of recurrent education will only be created when public examinations taken at school have been diminished in importance.

Even those who are successful in the academic hurdle

race are damaged from the point of view of a recurrent programme. Howard Becker points out in an essay entitled 'School is a Lousy Place to Learn Anything in' that 'Schools divorce themselves from the problems of the everyday world in an effort to make learning easier. They thus create a need for evaluative mechanisms and this diverts student effort from learning to efforts to be evaluated more highly.'[23] Curiosity and the desire to learn are replaced by the need to pass examinations. The satisfaction of intellectual achievement for its own sake is replaced by the need to satisfy the examiner. The tendency is for subjects which have been introduced to the curriculum, supposedly to liberalize examination-dominated courses, to become themselves examinable in order to guarantee student motivation and increase the number of examination passes. There can be no doubt that examinations do provide motivation for the successful school pupil, just as they reinforce failure for many of the others; but the natural desire of clever pupils to pass examinations would become an internal motivator of a limited and specific kind in any programme of educational opportunities devised in a lifelong perspective. Many teachers themselves have become conditioned by the examination system to regard all education goals in terms of papers to be answered. They have come to believe in new and different examinations as radical solutions to educational problems.

In making the case against examinations the following points require emphasis. Examinations do not do justice to the legitimate goals of a general or liberal education, because they measure those things which are the least important. Assessment through examinations has become linked, not with diagnosis of individual strength or weakness, or recommendation for further learning, but with stratification: pupils are placed in an order of merit for the external purposes of employers or institutions of higher education. Connected with this is the emphasis of public examinations on failure. Without failure examinations could not be efficient as a selection device, but that very failure early in many people's lives ensures that they will not gladly return to learning at later stages. In short, examinations help to prevent the lifelong dimension of recurrent education.

It would not be fair or accurate to single out secondary education and public examinations as the only barriers to a system of lifelong, mass educational opportunities. Much of the pressure on secondary education has come from the universities, which have encouraged many of those educational practices inimical to the lifelong processes of recurrent education.

Tyrell Burgess, in *Education after School*, makes a valuable distinction when he talks about the 'autonomous' and 'service' traditions in British education.[24] The autonomous tradition typified by the universities is aloof, exclusive, conservative and academic. Universities are independent of direct public intervention and are not obliged to respond to social pressures. They consider themselves to be engaged in the pursuit of learning for its own sake. They are self-justifying and not directly involved in professional or vocational education. On the other hand, the service tradition is responsive, open, innovatory and vocational. This is typified according to Burgess by the further education colleges and polytechnics. The development and division of these two separate traditions has affected schools as well. The autonomous tradition in schooling running from the nineteenth-century public school to the grammar school is still strong in today's comprehensive school. Comprehensive reorganization might have been expected to produce schools which graded the labour pool more finely, but heads of schools still have a great deal of autonomous independence.[25] Recent moves to assert the service function of schools have met with great resistance. The Taylor Committee recommendations on school governors,[26] and the review bodies which operate on a national basis, particularly those concerned with standards like the Assessment of Performance Unit, may begin to break down secondary school autonomy.

The Training Services Agency, in collaboration with local education authorities, is investigating what skills industry wants the schools to provide, and such projects may bring a service perspective into schools.[27]

Yet the autonomous school today is still largely sacred ground. John Methven, Director-General of the Confederation of British Industry, asked: 'How do you make the education service more accountable to the needs of the customer and consumer and, dare I say it, more accountable to society without compromising the traditional independence of the teacher and the profession?'[28] The mythical bogeyman of the clockwork, controlled French system in which, it is asserted, everyone does the same part of the same subject at the same time, is brandished whenever interference with the profession is threatened.

Schools claim to offer all their pupils a non-vocational education in the autonomous tradition; but in fact, as they are well aware, much of the assessment of their pupils' performance on non-vocational courses is used to select people for occupations. Universities are similarly involved in certification, though they cling more fiercely than schools to the value of the academic discipline for its own sake. For most university students, as for pupils at school, the courses they are following are of less significance than the qualifications at the end. Whereas in the 1920s and 1930s clever young men, even future Prime Ministers like Alec Douglas-Home, were content to come down from university with third-class degrees, having experienced to the full the creative milieu of the university, the struggle is now to achieve the good degree. This is a double failure. Because of the pressures to achieve successful qualification, the university can no longer succeed in educating in the widest sense, through the experience of the university as much as of the course itself; but because, at the same time, universities cling to the myth of education for its own sake, they refuse to align courses to follow these vocational needs directly. There are, in addition, a large number of unquestioned educational assumptions inherent in all university degree courses. What constitutes a degree? What level of work is degree level? What should be specified for entrants? What understanding of science, for example, is needed by someone who wishes to take a science degree?

The autonomous tradition has tremendous status, and this, feeding from universities into schools, deeply affects the whole education system. Burgess puts forward the idea of 'academic drift' to describe the tendency for institutions to attempt movement away from the service sector and towards autonomy.[29] His prime examples are the polytechnics, which often attempt to hive off their craft training functions to colleges of further education, and to take on degree-level courses. This leads to a constant battle to retain a strong service function in the teeth of staff desire for the status of autonomy. A peculiarly British snobbery, attached to the notion of usefulness in education, prevails even in the so-called binary system of higher education. But to argue against it is not to attack the idea of the university.

Autonomous educational institutions are necessary in a democratic society. An important part of any conceivable education system in Britain will be independent institutions which are creating new knowledge and teaching at a high level, without the constraints of the social/industrial/political establishment. But the key to a recurrent education system, providing mass education, will be the development in much greater numbers of service institutions, which respond to people and to their need to manage their lives within the constraints of their own social/industrial/political backgrounds and aspirations. These will not be more institutions of learning but institutions which learn. The service perspective is even more important in an age of rapid change. It is the task of recurrent education to develop institutions which are not only capable of providing the kind of opportunities that can be foreseen and outlined in a book such as this but also the kind of opportunities which no one can envisage at present. When Donald Schon wrote about institutions as 'memorials to past problems', and their 'dynamic conservatism' by which they struggle to retain their shape even when their original function has disappeared, he might have had British secondary schools in mind.[30] The desperate attempt to devise industrial studies examination syllabuses, in order to meet industrial criticisms of schools, is a recent example of dynamic conservatism. Through another academic examination schools hope to avoid providing a direct service and to retain their autonomy, while seeming to be flexible. In fact they will just be overloading the syllabus even more. By comparison the service institutions are used to devising courses, adapting to changing needs, and it is in the service sector that the models for a recurrent education future must lie.

The present further and higher education system is not a pattern of opportunities, it is a hierarchy and a ladder of esteem. To find genuinely open opportunities for the continuing education of adults one must look at the educational fringes. Of all these fringe areas only the Open University is really academically respectable, and even this is the result of a hard-fought struggle. It is significant that its courses are largely of degree level, that the institution is a university and that research functions have gradually been introduced. But as an extension of university work the Open University is of marginal importance, in terms of mass continuing education. Its exciting prospects lie in its non-degree and post-experience courses which use the same resources and distance-learning techniques as the degree courses. For these are imbued with the notion of service. Where traditional universities have developed a degree of service through their 'extra-mural' work, it rarely means what the Latin phrase implies – 'beyond the walls'; there is in only a few cases a real move to reach out and put the university's resources at the service of the community. Even where the university uses its own staff for courses outside the institution, they usually merely export the academic values and attitudes of the university in a watered-down form. As yet, most universities do not expect to apply their considerable expertise to the possible educational solutions of problems of technological and social change, as faced by local people in local organizations. They expect to provide, not to seek out, educational opportunities.

Other providers of adult education, in particular local education authorities, are only slowly moving away from their own form of autonomy towards a servicing function. In any contest over resources, however, adult education still comes last, since it has virtually no statutory support. Only a tiny proportion of the £6,000m. education budget, a sum less than the margin of error accepted in drawing up that budget, is devoted to adults in local authority adult education. Yet adults represent the majority of the population, and there has been a steady increase in adult student numbers since the Second World War, arising in part from the long-term effects of the lengthening of the school career. In the last three or four years a large number of authorities have even reduced their commitment, and in many authorities the annual increase in student numbers has ceased, as financial pressures have drastically raised fee levels. Even among its own professionals adult education is a service that thinks small. The Russell Report desired expansion from two to four million students in adult education, but there are over twenty-five million adults in the country, a great number of whom can be regarded as casualties of the examination dominated secondary system.[81]

In future chapters we shall look at the alternatives offered by recurrent education, and the way in which the three different functions of public examinations – education, qualification and selection – can each be performed much more satisfactorily by being treated separately. The only achievement of comprehensive secondary education so far is parity of esteem for 11-year-olds. Recurrent education insists that this is only the start of comprehensive education for all people at any age. We need parity of esteem and equal opportunities for learning at 16, at 18, at 21 and at every age up to 90 and over.

References

1 For a comparative approach see J. Simpson, *Today and Tomorrow in European Adult Education* (see note 12 to Chapter 1). For the British evidence, see J. Trenamen, 'Education in the Adult Population', *Adult Education*, vol. 30, no. 3, 1957.

2 G. Oakes, 'Policies and Priorities in Adult Education', *Adult Education*, vol. 51, no. 2, July 1978, p. 79, commenting on *Higher Education into the 1990s – A Discussion Document*, London, HMSO, Department of Education and Science, February 1978.

3 *Adult Education and National Development,* Occasional Paper No. XV, Commonwealth Foundation, p. 9.

4 H. Morris, 'The New Senior School in Britain' (see note 12 to Chapter 3).

5 D. E. Billing, 'A Review of the Literature concerning Methods of Selecting Students for Higher Education', *Durham Research Review*, no. 31, Autumn 1973, pp. 827–38.

6 *Higher Education: Report of the Committee appointed by the Prime Minister under the Chairmanship of Lord Robbins* (The Robbins Report), London, HMSO, 1963, appendix 2B, p. 409.

7 From Open University statistics on *Admissions.*

8 From Open University *Recognition* leaflets.

9 B. E. Coates and E. M. Rawstron, *Regional Variation in Britain*, London, Batsford, 1971, ch. 10.

10 A. K. Holliday and R. Maskill, *Entry to Chemistry Courses at Tertiary Level – a Preliminary Survey,* London, The Royal Society, 1972.

11 L. Ziliacus, 'Examinations', *New Era*, March–April 1934, p. 61, quoted in F. C. Happold, *Citizens in the Making*, London, Christophers, 1935.

12 B. S. Bloom *et al., A Taxonomy of Educational Objectives: the Classification of Educational Goals. Handbook 1*

Cognitive Domain, Handbook 2 Affective Domain,
London, Longman, 1965.

13 E. de Bono, in the *Guardian*, 4 May 1976, p. 7.

14 I. Illich, *After Deschooling, What?*, Cuernavaca, Social
Policy Inc., 1973, p. 50.

15 Quoted in J. Graves, *Policy and Progress in Secondary
Education 1902–42*, London, Nelson, 1943, p. 205. The
1917 Circular also suggested that the form and not the
pupil would be the unit for examination, and that it was
expected that a large proportion of the pupils in the form
should be able to satisfy the test.

16 *Curriculum and Examinations in Secondary Schools,*
Report of the Committee of the Secondary Schools
Examination Council (Norwood Report), London, HMSO,
1943, pp. 26–7.

17 E. de Bono, *Teaching Thinking*, London, Temple Smith,
1976, p. 13.

18 I. Berg, *Education and Jobs: The Great Training
Robbery*, Harmondsworth, Penguin, 1973, p. 35.

19 Ibid, chs. 6 and 7.

20 Dore, *The Diploma Disease*, pp. 23–4 (see note 6 to
Chapter 1).

21 *Young School Leavers*, Schools Council Enquiry No. 1,
London, 1968.

22 F. Musgrove, *Preliminary Studies of a Technological
University*, Bradford University, 1967, p. 20.

23 H. Becker, 'School is a Lousy Place to Learn Anything in',
in Blanche Geer (ed.), *Learning to Work*, Contemporary
Social Science Issues, Beverly Hills, SAGE, 1973, p. 101.

24 T. Burgess, *Education after School*, Harmondsworth, Penguin, 1977, p. 20.

25 J. Floud and A. H. Halsey, 'English Secondary Schools and
the Supply of Labour', in A. H. Halsey, J. Floud and C. A.
Andersen (eds), *Economy, Education and Society*, New
York, Free Press, 1961.

26 *A New Partnership for our Schools*, Report of a Committee of Enquiry . . . under the Chairmanship of Mr Tom
Taylor CBE (The Taylor Report), London, HMSO, 1977.

27 Reported in *The Times Educational Supplement*, 10 June
1977, p. 9. Followed up in *Manpower Services on Mersey-*

side, Report of the Merseyside Steering Group, Manpower Services Commission, December 1977, ch. 4.

28 J. Methven, 'What Industry Wants', *The Times Educational Supplement,* 29 October 1976, p. 2.

29 Burgess *Education after School*, p. 31 (see note 24 above).

30 D. A. Schon, *Reith Lecture No. 2.* See *Beyond the Stable State*, ch. 2 (see note 27 to Chapter 3).

31 *Adult Education: a Plan for Development* (The Russell Report), London, HMSO, 1973, p. x.

Chapter 5

Education across the Barriers

The obstacles to recurrent education exist in many areas of life and society, not just in the established views and expectations of schools and universities. Many people may accept the case for recurrent education as it affects the timing and prolongation of educational opportunities but recoil from the implications of recurrent education for the changed content of those opportunities. Yet the horizontal or life-wide dimension of recurrent education is as important as, and inseparable from, its vertical or lifelong dimension. A recurrent system has to cross the artificial barriers which we have all been conditioned to place around education, and in particular to break down the crumbling but still powerful apartheid which exists between education and training. We have argued in Chapter 3 that a smooth transition between earning and learning is desirable at all ages. This is the essential premise of the 'horizontal' dimension of recurrent education, and this emphasis on the link between education and the work-place is what separates modern notions of recurrent education from those visions of lifelong education which can be traced in British adult education back to 1919 and even earlier.

Education and training represent two intertwined branches of socialization. Together they provide the basis of a mature and stable personal identity, able to cope with the pressure of modern life. A fragmentation of the socialization process must occur when they are split. In Britain today there is a deep administrative and conceptual split between education and training. A recurrent education system would not divide experiences of personal development in this way. It would bring together and unify them. It would expect educators to accept some responsibility for the breadth as well as the length of life.

There are areas of life other than work which apply to recurrent education in this horizontal dimension. Education for leisure is already accepted, together with health education, sex education, education for family life and education for citizenship, as legitimate areas of concern for both adult educators and schoolteachers. A recurrent education system might want to place more emphasis, or a different emphasis, on the scope and timing of these areas of learning, but the seeds of growth in those fields already exist. There is no major obstacle, as there is with the notion of work-based education. Hence this chapter will concentrate on the relationship between education and work. Present distinctions between education and training ensure that during the working lives of most men and women their only significant learning experiences will be characterized by the providers, and perceived by themselves, as somehow different from education. This is a result of historical snobberies and modern inertia, and is the fault of both education and industry. With the formation of the Manpower Services Commission and its Training Services Division (previously the Training Service Agency), the administrative distinctions have become even more clear. A national training organization with regional hierarchies has come into existence in parallel with the education system. Yet, paradoxically, the educational or content distinctions have become even more blurred as the Training Services Division has felt the need to move its operations into the education field. For example, in some ways it is the Manpower Services Commission and the Training Services Division which have taken the lead and are beginning to put forward programmes for the 16–19 age group. These agencies are moving from their concern with training to consider quite naturally the general development of trainees.

The prevailing attitudes of educational institutions – especially schools and universities – to industry and the world of work is linked with a long, élitist tradition in which the 'educated' minority tended to find their careers in public service, including imperial administration, the Army and the Church, rather than in industry or commerce. Not surprisingly, these attitudes, reflecting, however unconsciously, the Victorian gentleman's ignorance and dislike of 'trade', have been much attacked recently by those concerned with the needs of industry. Targets have ranged from standards in literacy and numeracy to the general attitude to industry which is developed in schools. Sir Arnold Weinstock is particularly forceful: 'There are so many bad teachers and so much junk comes out of training colleges. Schools should concentrate their efforts on giving young people the skills for life.' He also produces arguments of accountability: 'I am in the business of paying for education and having to make use of its products. It is my right to complain. Education has fallen on its face and is getting worse.'[1] John Methven, Director-General of the Confederation of British Industry, makes the same point more politely: 'Among the various calls which are invariably made on education, the needs of the economy for manpower must stand high.'[2]

Sir Alex Smith, Director of Manchester Polytechnic and Chairman of the Schools Council, is concerned with the imbalance within the education system which leads students away from 'the ways in which the country earns its living'.[3] A *Guardian* schools essay competition in 1977, and again in 1978, produced evidence to support these fears. Industry was generally regarded by secondary pupils, according to the summary, as 'ugly, noisy, dirty, dangerous, dreary, monotonous, repetitive, soul-destroying, inhuman, insecure, underpaid and strike ridden'. One entrant wrote that 'The word [industry] fills me with dread.'[4] This dread is widespread and is affecting student choices of courses. Sir Alex Smith quotes enrolment figures: 'In advanced courses in Further Education, for every new student enrolling in 1973 to study production engineering, there were five in economics, twelve in law, sixteen in sociology and forty in business and commerce.'[5] The same kind of imbalance exists at earlier stages in education. During the 1960s the percentage of those taking A levels who opted for a Mathematics and Science combination dropped from 42.8 in 1963 to 30.9 in 1969, and the decline continued into the 1970s. In 1970 the percentage was 30.9 and in 1976, 26.6. This general decline took place against an overall increase in the numbers taking A levels.[6] A kind of personal academic drift is taking place which mirrors the institutional drift already described. Higher status accrues to those studying liberal arts subjects.

This particular educational pattern is of course self-perpetuating. High ability school pupils who contemplate higher or further education will naturally take their adult models from their teachers at school – who have, in most cases, themselves only had experience of the traditional routes of higher education. It has been suggested that industry does not try hard enough to woo the able young person. But it would take a great deal of effort on industry's part to counterbalance this tacit acceptance among school staff of the superiority of traditional academic routes and of liberal higher education. Thus attitudes hostile to industry, and indeed to work itself, are perpetuated, even in an age of mass secondary education that was barely contemplated by the genteel Victorian élite which originally created them. The British education system, with these prejudices and pre-occupations, has been widely imitated in many other countries of the former Empire. Ronald Dore has described some of the distortions which this causes.[7] Correlli Barnett points out some of the problems for India in his *Collapse of British Power*. Nineteenth-century higher education in India was modelled on the British system, and as a result it produced, 'not the engineers, scientists and technicians which India needed with its lack of industry and its desperately backward agriculture, but unemployables of "liberal" education, good at best for low grade clerking, but believing themselves to be a deprived élite – apt material for political dreaming and scheming'.[8]

In the late 1970s we see in Britain the effects of the continuous defeat, in a long struggle lasting throughout this century, of those who wished the schools to be more concerned with vocational preparation. In 1895 the Bryce Commission, the report of which is generally attributed to the eminent educationist M. Sadler, wrote that 'Secondary education is the education of the boy or girl not simply as a human being who needs to be instructed in certain rudiments of knowledge, but it is a process of intellectual training and personal discipline conducted with special regard to the profession or trade to be followed.'[9] Similarly, the *Board of Education Report, 1913–14* suggested that 'All school work may in some sense be regarded as vocational in that it should be planned with regard to the probable future of the pupils.'[10] The First World War and the introduction of a state examination system reduced the urgency of employers' demands which had produced this statement. Lindsay, in 1926, demanded a more broadly constructive attitude: 'So long as schools exist, and every decade they are multiplied, they must stand in some more intimate relation both with work and the outside world and with the advances which are made in social and economic life and modern thought.'[11] He also saw the crucial importance of careful vocational guidance: ' "Discovery classes" between 14 and 16 are more humane and economical than "recovery classes" between 16 and 18.'[12] Percy, in 1933, continued the theme of vocational preparation:

the brute truth is that while Pascal said long ago, a man's choice of his trade is the most important thing in his life, this crucial choice is about the one thing for which our public system of education has made hardly any attempt to prepare its pupils. Ever since the Factory Acts we have been obsessed by the dangers which attend the entry of young people into what is called 'organized industry'. Yet broadly speaking we have been content to dam back the flow of juvenile labour into industry by an embankment built up to a legal level . . . The more ardently we argue about the raising of the school leaving age the less do we apparently concern ourselves with the subsequent helter skelter rush of those barraged waters over the countryside below.[13]

Frank Musgrove pointed out the continuing truth of all these earlier observations in the 1970s.[14] He suggests that the concept of adolescence as a period of confusion, of stress and of testing values and attitudes is an illusion. He stresses the certainty and the ease with which young people move into adult roles when this is permitted. Occupational choice is seen as the crucial experience of this adult status. But vocational preparation for adolescents is not considered an important role of the school. The debate still goes on. The Newsom Report expected the schools to deal with a general preparation for occupation rather than any specific job:

Probably at first boys and girls only think of a subject as vocational if it involves learning to do something like brick-laying, which is part of the way people earn a living and which is not related to school work as they have hitherto known it. They can see the point of a vocational subject and often enjoy it whether they themselves are going to take up this kind of work or not.[15]

The Report goes on to suggest that a vocational interest would support the normal curriculum: 'Ordinary school work becomes vocational.'

Such a tone is usual in national reports and betrays a confusion of thought with regard to vocational studies. Ideas of education as a national investment and as a source of trained manpower are accepted. Lip service is paid to the idea (in the case of Newsom with regard to the low ability child) of preparing the young worker. But, other than stressing practical studies and concern for guidance, educators refuse to cross the line and say schools should, as part of their function, be concerned with vocational preparation.

The Training Services Agency paper *The Vocational Preparation of Young People* suggests that schools should 'prepare young people for the patterns of behaviour that will be expected of them at work'.[16] Yet an analysis of the paper published in *Secondary Education* felt that 'Although it would be absurd to suggest that young people should not conform to industrial discipline there can be no doubt that schools must give overriding consideration to the personal development of their pupils.'[17]

This is a modern echo of what Robert Morant must have felt when he opposed Sadler's views of secondary education in the influential Education Act of 1902, i.e. that personal development is somehow a separate consideration from preparation for work. But the truth is, as Sadler wrote for the Bryce Report, that secondary education and preparation for work ('technical instruction' is how he puts it) differ only as 'genus and species, or as general term and particular name'.[18] If a child leaves school without the ability to manage the next stage of his life, there can be no doubt that the school has not served him well and has disregarded an important part of his personal development. Vocational preparation may not be the most important aspect of a secondary-school curriculum; but unless it is there, alongside the more traditional concerns of a general education base, the fragmentation of socialization will continue to hamper the development of recurrent education, and consequently of mature individuals able to cope with the rapid changes in their lives. Today the debate over vocational preparation is fuelled by the pressure on training agencies and their personnel to produce the skilled men required for Britain's economic future.

It is the pattern of change which now makes this whole debate urgent. In Sadler's time it was acceptable, if not altogether true, to argue that school was the time for learning, for acquiring an education, and the rest of life would be spent working or in retirement. The cosy three-stage life – school, work, retirement – has been shattered. To enter work, yet not to have completed one's education, is the

norm today, whether 16-year-olds and their teachers realize
it or not. Even the genus–species analogy is outdated. In
Sadler's time the genus was education and the species technical instruction, both clearly definable. Today the typology
has to be changed to allow for species yet to be discovered
in the light of future technological change. The genus has
become learning skills in general, while the species include
all specific subject areas from Classics to Computer Technology, Mathematics to Welding. There should be no aristo-
crats, no middle class and no 'untouchables' in this race.

For many educators this fusion of education with training
remains incomprehensible. They retreat behind the intellectual barricades of an argument about 'high standards', not
recognizing that high standards are essential to all forms of
learning. This recognition that high standards can exist in
every branch of education must provide the basis of any
system of mass, comprehensive education. Another, more
philosophical, argument claims that education has no ends
other than those which it prescribes for itself, whereas training is undergone on behalf of outside agencies. But it is only
a narrow segment of education which is concerned with
its own intrinsic ends. For most people, in most forms of
education, their engagement in it is a means to an end, as
the Schools Council Enquiry No. 1 showed so graphically.[19]
In a sense all forms of education are a means to an end. In
one form or other they will all lead to the end of personal
development, of an awareness of oneself or one's society.
There is no reason except snobbery to assume extra merit, or
demerit, in purely academic learning or in those forms of
knowledge which have no obvious practical value.

Another argument used is that the content of training,
quite apart from its purpose, involves none of the powers of
thought and use of critical, questioning faculties which
characterize the content of education. This, too, is an outdated notion. In an age of worker participation, of job
enrichment schemes and of advanced technology, there is
only a very limited number of unskilled work activities

which can be learnt by rote or by 'sitting next to Nellie'.
Moreover, even those unskilled activities which will persist
for the foreseeable future can be the basis of a liberal or
general education in the right teaching hands. In parts of
West Germany all young workers take part in a compulsory
day-release scheme until they are 18. In the *Berufsschulen*,
the institutions in which this is carried out, programmes of
education are built around the students' occupation.[20] It is
possible to use low-grade unskilled occupations as a
springing-off point for a programme of continuing general
education. With especially designed courses there is no
reason why older, as well as younger, workers should not
receive educational opportunities that are based on the jobs
they do.

To break down the present duality of education and training will require the support of employers and industry as well
as teachers and the education system. Despite the criticism
heaped on to schools in recent years there can be as much
blame attached to industry as to education for the existing
system. For a very long time firms ignored the content of
the secondary school curriculum, abandoned any responsibility for selecting their employees and simply used the
approximate and inappropriate grading devices supplied by
the system of academic examinations. Such laziness and
indifference to the school syllabus on the part of employers
is proving an embarrassment to them now that the extension
of educational opportunities immediately after school leaves
them with a rump of 16-year-olds less able than they had
become accustomed to attract. Moreover, even though they
ask for it in schools, many firms have been slow to provide
their own form of vocational preparation. The bulk of
industry's efforts in this field is concentrated on the induction
and training of skilled workers, but even in this apparently
vital survival activity the record of industry as a whole is not
good. Some employers have taken a great deal of persuading
to carry out any of their own training, and the poaching of
skilled men by firms who do no training themselves is still

widespread.[21] In 1977 and 1978 firms were stating that a shortage of skilled labour was an important factor limiting their development.[22] It appears that this factor has been a problem since at least 1960.[23] Firms tend to cut training and recruitment drastically and quickly during periods of recession. If training programmes are abandoned or reduced in this way, the inevitable time lag in the production of skilled men will result in a shortage of skill when economic life quickens. The 1964 Industrial Training Act and the formation of training boards with their levy/grant system could not overcome this problem, because the firms still assessed their own needs for labour. It is only since the 1973 Act and the formation of the Manpower Services Commission and its Training Division that large-scale measures have been possible to smooth out the supply of skilled labour. There are now Training Award schemes in operation which take on apprentices and train them, away from firms. The numbers taken on depend on an assessment of the shortfall in industry's recruitment. The Training Services Division and the industrial training boards have had to devise such schemes to save firms from themselves.

Frequently the unions need convincing that changes in the traditional routes to skilled status are not a threat. A natural desire to preserve employment for their members has made the lower echelons of the craft unions resistant to the notion of retraining for skilled status in Skillcentre short courses, to any sort of accelerated training, or to the idea that skilled status should be awarded after skill tests, rather than after serving a particular length of time. Apprenticeship has always had several different purposes. It is a pattern of training which produces skilled men for an employer. It is also the means by which an individual learns a craft which is usable in an entire industry. But it can also be seen as a means of limiting access to skilled status, and thus a way of retaining job status, high employment and good wages.

The way in which British industry has handled the induction and training of skilled men gives little cause for pride, but the picture, as far as those outside the circle of skill are concerned, is even blacker. For the unskilled and semi-skilled the problem is not one of poor induction and training but one of hardly any induction and training at all. Most employers limit their vocational preparation in this area to the essential training required to do the job.

Industry might ask for vocational preparation in schools but its own provision of initial training is still poor. The Henniker–Heaton Report in 1964 asked for a doubling of the number of those under 18 receiving training on a part-time basis to 500,000 by 1970. In fact the number receiving training of this type had shrunk from 269,030 in 1965 to 243,945 in 1970, and to 169,698 by 1975. Seen as a percentage of those youngsters actually employed there was little change from 1964 to 1970.[24] During the 1970s government intervention has been necessary in order that training is seen as a vehicle for the long-term needs of young workers, rather than just a way of meeting the short-term requirements of the firm. Of course, as we have suggested earlier, the *long-term* needs of the firm and the individual are in fact closely intertwined.

Most of the stimulus behind the range of Manpower Services Commission schemes of vocational preparation and work experience has undoubtedly been the high proportion of those aged under 20 who are unemployed. But, whatever the initial stimulus, there is now some commitment to schemes of further education for all young workers. Schemes of Unified Vocational Preparation (UVP) have been put forward and pilot projects are in operation. In the foreword to the government statement on UVP, the four Secretaries of State involved say: 'We believe that properly conceived vocational preparation at this crucial stage would not only raise the economic contribution of these young people but would enhance their chances for development in a personal as well as a vocational sense.'[25]

Industry is even more backward with regard to the con-

inuing education of its more mature workers. In Britain
he notion of paid educational leave, as developed abroad
and supported by the International Labour Organization, is
rarely invoked by either side of industry, though limited
encouragement for education does exist in the more enlightened organizations.

British industry is a long way from accepting what is an
obvious and necessary quid pro quo in the context of recurrent education. Schools will have to modify their curricula to facilitate ease of transition to work; but industry
will have to allow paid educational leave for all forms of
education, even those where there is no direct link with the
work of the firm. If schools are to be openly concerned with
manpower as well as manhood, it follows that industry
must accept responsibility for the further individual development of employees, whatever form it takes, as well as their
own needs for skilled manpower. At present, if schools provide work-experience schemes, they tend to be for the least
able, those not taking examinations, and therefore to be
regarded as a fringe activity. In some schools work experience is seen simply as a way of removing 'problems' from the
school campus. The contrast provided by the current practice of paid educational leave is predictable. In those few
professions where employees are released for their own
personal choice of educational course, the recipients of this
leave tend to be those who have already received the most
education in childhood. Teachers on secondment are perhaps the most obvious example. In any recurrent system
both these processes – work-experience schemes at school
and paid educational leave at work – would be vastly extended at all levels of ability and for all types of learning.

Strangely, British industry also seems to accept the valua-
tion which education has placed upon it. For instance, while
schools are no doubt to blame for not creating an atmosphere
which encourages pupils to enter production engineering,
this does not explain why the rewards are so low for those
who do. In general all those working in manufacturing

industries are poorly rewarded by comparison with service industries or government. In 1976 only 3.0 per 1,000 employees in manufacturing industries earned over £8,500 compared with 4.4 in education, 5.0 in local authorities and 17.0 in banks and insurance.[26]

Both education and industry are to blame, therefore, for the separateness and inadequacies of education and training, and there are many people on both sides of the fence who will want to keep them apart. Young people have direct experience of this apartheid when they come into contact with the School Careers Service. Here, where the worlds of education and work should be intertwined, the school pupil is all too often faced with totally inadequate advice and preparation. Careers education is the poor relation of the education service. According to the Training Services Agency, 'The short-comings of careers education in schools makes the work of the careers officer more difficult. The Careers service is spread thinly over the school population and, because of this, it often has less influence on job choice than parents, relatives and friends.'[27] It is essential that occupational choice should be the result of a programme of career development starting early in the secondary school and based on some practical experience of the atmosphere, requirements and discipline of the work-place. But this kind of detailed programme would make inroads into the traditional curriculum and time-table, especially if high ability children were to benefit: 'It is the system that is at fault not the teachers. The emphasis on the academic tradition means that the job of the careers teachers, although increasing in importance, still has little recognition.'[28] There can be no justification for a careers advice and guidance system which fails children. A Leicestershire working party on education and industry investigated the transition from school to work in conjunction with the Training Services Agency: 62 per cent of those questioned as they began work felt that the last year at school had provided no useful preparation; one interviewee said that 'The last year at school was not useful because of exams. Fourth year was better than fifth – had more trips and visits – slackened off in the fifth year because of exams.'[29]

Working together with common aims would benefit educational institutions, employers and the individual learner. Attempts to work together have not always been successful, perhaps because the prevailing ethos of separation has been dominant in the minds of all concerned. For instance, the sandwich course in universities has been introduced to produce a proper awareness of the outside world, but it seems to come too late to produce any real fusion of theory and practice. Technology students at Bradford University were 'disappointed by the hiatus between university and industrial experience'. They 'were concerned at the disruption of university studies'. They did not see it as a time for applying theory in practice or as a good time for finding out about career opportunities.[30] Some universities and polytechnics are attempting to provide an interpenetration of education and industry, but at that stage the opportunities for success are limited. The problem is too deep-rooted. There is no status, no sense of self-esteem, involved in sandwich courses, because there is no status in any education which relates closely to work. This problem is seen at all levels of education and is reflected in polarities familiar in educational debate – vocational versus non-vocational, pure versus applied, even arts versus science. Sir Alex Smith has pointed out that a symbol of the imbalance lies in the two national reports produced in 1964 – the Robbins Report on universities and the Henniker–Heaton Report on day release. Whereas there has been a colossal expansion in the availability of full-time higher education, the numbers obtaining day release have decreased.[31] A bilateral system of higher education has been created with status and resources unevenly spread between the two sectors.

In practice, training has a great deal to offer education. For some time the best industrial trainers have used systems derived from ideas of curriculum development which originated in educational theory. Beginning with an analysis of the job, its place in the overall work of the company, they specify training needs in behavioural terms, and determine the best training strategy (on-the-job or off-the-job training, for example). They assess the value of their chosen programme by a pre-test and a post-test, and use the information they gather to decide how the next training programme needs to be changed. With the terminology changed, this would be an ideal way to devise educational programmes. It is a technique used by some staff in some colleges of further education. But, unlike most staff in 'educational' institutions, the trainer is concerned with success: he aims to train *all* his intake to the required level. He works to what is called the 90/90 rule. It is intended that 90 per cent of the students should score 90 per cent in any test. A trainer who worked to a constant failure rate of 30–40 per cent would be wasting a great deal of his firm's time and money. Might it not be that an education system which does just this also wastes time and money?

The kind of behavioural objectives which are applicable in training might be too limiting in some educational spheres. There must be room for incidental learning: many educational engagements will quite properly be voyages into the unknown. Nevertheless, for many teachers the attempt to define in explicit terms the objectives of the courses they teach (other than to get them through the examination!) would be a salutary exercise. For all teachers to consider, in advance and in detail, what their pupils should learn rather than what the teacher knows how to teach, would be an invigorating process and a reversal of what is too frequently the teaching mode.

Education has a great deal to offer training as well. For a start it can help to make real the avowed objectives of training courses. The Manpower Services Commission obviously feels already that its work has greater scope than that normally attributed to training: 'Training helps the performance of the individual, and collectively, the performance of the firm. But it also helps to develop the individual potential and allows the worker to get more out of life.'[32] Many trainers need in-service education, and it is a peculiarity of modern language usage that teachers tend to talk about their 'in-service training' while policemen, magistrates and shop stewards receive 'role education'. It is time that policy and educated attitudes caught up with this promiscuous use of 'training' and 'education' in common parlance. Training and education are very close relatives in the same family, not inhabitants of separate planets.

Although we are suggesting that education should have a greater service role and develop a much closer relationship with the world of industry, this is not putting education at the service of industry. By developing a closer relationship between earning and learning, within the school programme as well as later on throughout the working life, it is possible to relate the manpower needs of industry to the personal development needs of individuals. It cannot be emphasized too often that it is a ridiculous exercise to attempt to separate the two. The Crowther Report made the point that:

> The education of the Nobel prizewinner is, by any test, a profitable investment for the community; there are many persons the justification for whose education must be sought almost entirely in what it does for them as individuals. But it is hard to tell which is which at the start, and not always easy later on. There are indeed parts of everybody's education which have no economic value, and there is nobody whose education is entirely without it.[33]

If the relationship of manpower and personal development needs is seen in a lifelong perspective, if vocational development is subsumed within the personal development goals of education, then the fear that vocational education merely fits people for restricted occupations evaporates. The definition of 'education' must be broadened to include vocational development and preparation; and it is equally important

that the concept of 'training' be brought within the educational family.[34]

References

1 Sir Arnold Weinstock, Address to Youth Charter Conference, 1977. Reported in *The Times Educational Supplement*, 11 February 1977, p. 8.
2 Methven, 'What Industry Wants' (see note 28 to Chapter
   4).
3 Sir Alex Smith. BBC 2 Broadcast on 11 January 1977.
4 The *Guardian*, 22 June 1977, pp. 18–19 and 6 July 1978,
   pp. 16–17.
5 Sir Alex Smith, (see note 3 above).
6 *Statistics of Education 1962–75: Vol. 1 Schools* London,
   HMSO.
7 Dore, *The Diploma Disease* (see note 6 to Chapter 1).
8 C. Barnett, *The Collapse of British Power,* London,
   Methuen, 1972, p. 140.
9 *The Bryce Commission Report,* C 7862, vol. VII, 1895, pp.
   135–6.
10 *Board of Education Report 1913–14*, Cmd. 7934, p. 95.
11 K. Lindsay, *Social Progress and Educational Waste,*
   London, G. Routledge & Sons, 1926, p. 28.
12 Ibid, p. 34.
13 Lord Percy, Preface (pp. v–vii) to B. A. Abbott, *Education for Commerce and Industry in England*, Oxford
   University Press, 1933.
14 Musgrove, 'Childhood and Adolescence' (see note 17 to
   Chapter 3).
15 *Half our Future: A Report of the Central Advisory Council for Education (England)* (The Newsom Report),
   London, HMSO, 1963, para 322, pp. 115–16.
16 *Vocational Preparation for Young People: A Discussion
   Paper*, Training Services Agency, Manpower Services Commission, 1975, p. 15.
17 J. Gennard. 'The TSA – an Appraisal', *Secondary Education,* vol. 6, no. 1, June 1976, pp. 8–10.

18 Quoted in J. Graves, *Policy and Progress in Secondary Education 1902–42*, p. 21 (see note 15 to Chapter 4).

20 See the *Guardian*, 2 March 1976, p. 17, for an account of one programme.

21 *Training for Vital Skills*, Training Services Agency Discussion Paper, Training Services Agency/Manpower Services Commission, June 1976.

22 Confederation of British Industry, *Trends in Industry*.

23 See the *Guardian*, 15 August 1978, p. 15, for an analysis of skill-shortage trends.

24 *Statistics of Education 1962–75: vol. III Further Education,* London, HMSO.

25 *Unified Vocational Preparation – A Pilot Approach,* London, HMSO, March 1976, p. 1.

26 The *Guardian*, 20 July 1976, p. 16.

27 *Vocational Preparation for Young People*, p. 16, para. 4.12 (see note 16 above).

28 Sir Edward Britten in evidence to the Education Sub-Committee of the House of Commons, reported in *The Times Educational Supplement*, 25 February 1977, p. 10.

29 E. T. Keil, *Becoming a Worker: Report of a Survey Financed by the Leicestershire Working Party on Education and Industry and by the TSA*, September 1976.

30 F. Musgrove, *Sandwich Course Studies*, Bradford University, 1970, p. 161.

31 Sir Alex smith (see note 3 above).

32 *The Manpower Services Commission – A Five Year Plan,* Manpower Services Commission, 1974, p. 1.

33 *15–18: A Report of the Central Advisory Council for Education (England)* (The Crowther Report), London, HMSO, 1959, p. 55, para. 86.

34 Allen Parrott, 'Lifelong Education and Training', *Adult Education*, vol. 48 no. 5, Jan. 1976, pp. 301–8.

Chapter 6

The Way Ahead: Strategy and Implications

The following three chapters suggest ways in which the themes explored so far might be translated into practice in Britain. The need is not to overturn the existing education system but to build on it. Extensive and even radical reforms in the education system could be brought about with minimum disruption if sufficient numbers of teachers and policymakers in all fields of education were made aware of those new contexts for their work which are implicit in the recurrent education idea. These contexts include new kinds of schooling, new approaches to post-school education and new professional attitudes. But, if the will exists, they can be achieved by a phased programme of gradual changes and improvements. The reforms described in these chapters are not dependent on the swing of the party political pendulum and need not therefore result in the same kinds of dispute as were provoked in many parts of the country by the introduction of comprehensive schools.

The recurrent education practices discussed in this chapter do not constitute a blueprint. It is ten years since Bertrand Schwarz estimated in some detail the cost of an imagined system of *l'education permanente* for France in the year 1985, and it was an interesting if optimistic exercise.[1] A blueprint for Britain, especially one with financial estimates, cannot be written with any degree of realism until a British government has committed the country to a coherent policy of reform and reallocation of resources in education. There is no sign of such new policies at the time of writing (1979), and the 'great debate' on education continues to consist of a debate about the education of children. On the other hand, there will be no policy moves in the direction of recurrent education unless a significant body of opinion can visualize its practical forms and are persuaded of its feasibility. The aim of this chapter, therefore, is not to portray the whole recurrent education edifice in great detail but to show the foundations and a few of its crucial building-blocks. The current debate about school curricula and school standards is limited and shortsighted. Recurrent education could add meaning to it by removing the mental barrier which assumes that education must forever equal schooling and can never be generally available after the adolescent years. In moving towards a recurrent education strategy three of the themes from earlier chapters need to be kept in mind. The first premise of recurrent education planning is the rejection of the time constraint on education provision. The second premise is a rejection of the narrow content assumptions and restrictions which traditionally underlie educational thinking. By extending both the time and the content components of education, a recurrent system would become the first major plan to come to grips with the problem of mass education. It would have the potential, which a child-centred system cannot have, of associating education in everyone's mind with the quality of life. It would have the potential, which an academic subject-dominated system cannot have, of appealing to all sorts and conditions of men. A third premise of recurrent education planning, which brings together the first two, is that the individual and social requirements from an education system are not incompatible.

Ian Lister doubts whether the individual and social requirements from an education system can be unified.[2] He asks a key question of all educational planners: 'whether their plans are economy-centred (based on projected manpower requirements) or man-centred (based on a vision of man)'. This polarized view, shared alike by conservatives and radicals, is rejected in recurrent education on grounds that are both pragmatic and idealistic. A 'vision of man' which excludes man the worker will lead to an education system which excludes a large part of people's identity and self-esteem from its focus. As we have already suggested, alienation from education is a great deal more striking in British society than alienation from work, and only by drawing closer to the economic structure can any education system hope to have an influence for the better. At the same time, any manpower plan which assumes that its sole concern is to put the right number of hands in the right place at the right time will certainly fail. The rigid programming of people for jobs makes no economic sense. Individuals, both as social animals and as workers, need today a broadness of education and a flexibility of approach to the range of new situations which they will inevitably encounter. To maintain an opposition between the noble (educational) goals of manhood and the sordid (training) goals of manpower is either an unwelcome legacy of a Victorian past, or a dubious enticement to a utopian future. There must be new attitudes on both sides. As educationists begin to understand that the work-place is as suitable an area for personal development as the classroom, so industry must accept that it is in its best interest to make the work-place as creative an area for personal development as possible.

A new willingness on the part of employers to change the pattern of people's working lives, so as to incorporate periodic breaks for educational experiences, will not require them to show an unlikely degree of altruism. It is in everyone's interest to reconcile economic needs and individual desires for personal renewal. Such a reconciliation, on the other hand, should not be sold to employers as a potentially fruitful equation of 'happy' workers and increased profits. The overall aim is less unhappiness and more fulfilment as human beings not just as workers; and in this particular context recurrent education is just one part of a threefold attempt to reduce that fragmentation of individual experience which is the consequence of separating work from the rest of life.

The other two aspects of this broad movement to remedy the worst psychological effects of the industrial revolution are job enrichment schemes and worker participation. The attempt to democratize control of the work-place and to involve employees, or their representatives, in the taking of policy decisions is not very far advanced in Britain. But the move towards worker participation is an international phenomenon and can be seen as a growing challenge to the status quo in all developed nations. It is also part of a wider political push towards decentralization and the devolution of power to more local groupings. Like recurrent education, the philosophical basis of worker participation is the desire to give individuals a greater degree of control in the management of their own lives, a greater say in the management of each particular facet of their environment.

'Job enrichment' is the third prong of this same humanizing movement. Just as one can imagine a time when the adjective 'recurrent' is redundant in the phrase 'recurrent education', because education will automatically be regarded as a lifelong activity, and a time when the word 'worker' will automatically embrace the notion of participating in decisions about work policies, so too can the word 'enrichment' be regarded as a temporary necessity when used in the phrase 'job enrichment'. All jobs should be designed with human dignity in mind. At present, job enrichment is the way in which some firms, usually in production and manufacturing industry, though the need is just as great in many service jobs, attempt to overcome the dullness and impersonal nature of much work activity. A key feature is often a reduction in the repetitiveness of tasks which have to be carried out in extremely short time cycles, sometimes less than ninety seconds per task, for many hours a day. Other features of job enrichment schemes include management by objectives, the introduction of flexi-time, a greater emphasis on health and safety and on ergonomic principles when designing work tasks, the use of autonomous work groups and the rotation of jobs. The novelty of modern job enrichment ideas lies in the refusal of many work reformers to accept the primacy of short-term profits as the major criterion of the successful organization. Treating their aims as long-term profitability and continuity, rather than year-by-year profits, allows enterprises to accommodate humane principles. This in turn helps them to sink roots which go deep enough to survive temporary periods of economic adversity. But the theoretical basis of job enrichment is not new. It was long ago expressed by Fourier, the early nineteenth-century socialist, when he wrote that 'Morality teaches us how to love work: let it know then how to render work lovable.'[3]

In the real world, therefore, there is an intimate connection between the notions of quality *of* life and chances *in* life. A recurrent education system would express this connection by linking educational opportunities with employment opportunities in particular, and with working life in general. In practice, this means that there would have to be an interpenetration of earning and learning opportunities at all stages of development, including not only the period now devoted to compulsory schooling, but also the various periods of adulthood and of working life. And a key strategy to achieve this interpenetration of education and work in adult life is paid educational leave (PEL). In 1980 there is due to be published a report on PEL from a research project funded by the Department of Education and Science.[4] At present the concept of PEL is given verbal support by government, and by official employer and union organizations. In practice, it is still largely confined to professional groups, such as teachers. Where it is more widely granted, almost without exception there are restrictions and limitations on the courses which employees are entitled to take. But in a recurrent education system adults must have freedom to follow courses of their own choice, irrespective of the needs of their employers. It is only the potential students themselves who can decide the most appropriate form of personal development at any particular stage of their lives, and any system of educational 'credits' must incorporate this free choice as a right, not a bargaining counter. The early 1980s will see whether or not British governments do more than pay lip service to PEL.

Equally important in the overall strategy of recurrent education is the close association of work and education during schooldays, making explicit in the curriculum of secondary education what is already implicit in the minds of pupils and their parents. If it were accepted that for young people valuable experiences of personal growth can take place in various controlled situations outside the school, many problems of secondary education would disappear. The arbitrary school-leaving age might be replaced with a more rational system in which the duration of adolescent education varied from individual to individual. At a certain point there would be no need for compulsory attendance. The young person would take over responsibility for his or her learning experiences. Continuity in education would be provided by the counselling arm of a recurrent education service, which would be guiding young people through the structured opportunities of their early education, and advising them on their later path through the opportunities of post-compulsory education. The pattern of the socialization process would not be the same for each individual child.

Adolescents would naturally spend a considerable amount of time in periods of controlled work experience as an integral part of their overall educational programme, and with no detriment to other parts of it, because of the extended time scale of recurrent education. Sophisticated vocational preparation, with carefully monitored work experience, would become a part of every young person's curriculum. This would ensure that education was seen to be related to the outside world, and would lay the foundation for the full exploitation of later educational opportunities in adult life. Foundation programmes of this kind for young people would reflect that balance between work and education which would be available to them throughout life.

The creation of educational institutions which can lead young people naturally into this world of post-school living and learning must be a priority in any recurrent education plan. People whose views of the education system are formed, or deformed, by their early school experiences will have no expectation of benefit from any recurrent education system which is simply grafted on top of a school-dominated status quo. If young people are unaffected in their schools by recurrent education, they will stay unaffected as adults. Adult educators have attempted for a long time, and with only limited success, to attract significant numbers of working-class students. Their efforts, even with increased resources, will continue to fail until schools recognize that they are the vital links between each growing child and the outside world. They must not be the funnel whereby some children are enabled to find an approved niche in society, while others, whether they sink or swim, are left with only bad memories of their seemingly finished education. A new approach to schooling is a prerequisite of successful recurrent education.

In considering the compulsory education sector as the early stage of an overall recurrent education system it may eventually make sense to discard the existing titles 'primary' and 'secondary'. They belong to an earlier age when it was a matter of some urgency to gain something more than the most basic education for as many children as possible. Today such terms encourage an unconscious identification of education with childhood, and an unstated assumption that two, or possibly three ('tertiary'), periods of learning will be the norm for a lifetime. In *Education Without Frontiers* Fragnière suggests that the terms 'compulsory' and 'exploratory' should denote education offered up to the age of 19.[5] 'Higher' education would be available for the rest of life, 'higher' regarded as synonymous with 'open'. Such adjectives are more in tune with recurrent education and may usefully be kept in mind, though in this chapter, for ease of understanding, we continue to use the terms 'school' and 'secondary school' to refer to the institutions which may in time develop from them.

The chief remedy which a recurrent system could offer secondary education for many of its current problems would be the separation of the various functions and objectives that are ineffectively fused together by the blunt instrument of external examinations. As we have tried to show, secondary schools attempt to achieve extensive and disparate goals with a curriculum which, despite constant and numerous modifications, remains at heart appropriate only to the more academically gifted pupils for whom it was in fact originally designed. Compulsory education in a recurrent system would have as its major function the provision of a general education for all children. This would include most obviously the basic tools of learning – literacy, numeracy and elementary communication skills. This goal – a universal general education for all children – would be treated separately from the needs of young people to gain useful qualifications, and from the needs of employers and higher education institutions to have young people graded for selection purposes.

Within the compulsory sector engaged in this basic function of general education, secondary schools would have the extra function of providing exploratory activities for all their pupils. These would be explorations either into academic subjects, or into work experience, or, most probably, a mixture of both. This programme of exploratory activity would contribute to the general education of each child, because every course would be designed to have an intrinsic value at the time it was being experienced. But it would also provide the route to qualifications. No course of study, whether academic or work-based, would be taken *in vacuo*, as a way of filling time for pupils, or time-tables for teachers. Every course for every pupil would have its educational justification. In practice, many courses would be devised as the result of a continuing process of consultation by schools both with higher education institutions and with employers. Such consultation would be of paramount importance to the course devisers, in order that they were known to be providing the background and preparation appropriate to each pupil's developing aspirations. The reason for working with all such agencies outside the school would be to ensure that every pupil was given the best possible opportunities in adolescence; it would not be to provide a system of grading pupils into successes and failures.

At any one time the objectives for each pupil in compulsory education should be both limited and explicit, not diffuse and unstated. The 'educated man', 'critical awareness', 'heightened sensibility', 'creative understanding' – these are goals appropriate to a lifetime of learning, not to a few crowded years of schooling. In a recurrent system gaps in any child's academic experiences could be made up in adulthood. With limited and explicit goals for each child in mind, the job of the schools would become easier. The school's objectives, too, would be much more limited: ensuring that every pupil was able to manage the period immediately after leaving school, whether at full-time work, full-time study or part-time work and study. At the same time, as part of an on-going process, the school would be making all pupils aware of the range of lifetime educational opportunities, and the certainty of their return to the student role at intervals in later life. Existing secondary schools can be seen as fixed moulds, turning out 'end-products' with their own built-in obsolescence. The institutions of adolescent education in a recurrent system would be concerned far more with building in the processes rather than the products of education. In these ways future adults would be prepared for adaptability in a world of change.

One obvious problem in practice will be agreement about the general education component in compulsory education. A core curriculum of basic knowledge alongside literacy and numeracy which could usefully be given to all pupils is a controversial notion. Yet if there is to be a lifelong series of paths through the institutions of a recurrent system, and eventually as many paths as there are children, it makes sense that at the start there should be some central core of basic learning skills on which they can build in later life. Each child should gain some experience at least of the various kinds of learning characterized in Bloom's taxonomy as 'cognitive', 'affective' and 'psycho-motor'.[6] This still leaves a great deal of scope when devising such a core curriculum. The immense advantage of recurrent education plans over reforms based entirely on the schools themselves is that arguments about the detailed content of a core curriculum will have been largely defused. There is no such thing in a recurrent system as 'sacrificing the future of our children'. Decisions about the core curriculum would not be irrevocable, and it may be that each school would solve the problem of general education in its own way, subject to some nationally prescribed guidelines.

Another problem is to visualize the nature of the individual routes through compulsory education. The recurrent education institution would offer a range of learning activities and programmes, which could be assembled in different ways to suit individual pupils. Alongside a core curriculum consisting of various learning skills would be a remedial service to deal with individual learning difficulties diagnosed from the core programmes or on other courses. Attached to this basic and central element of adolescent education would be a number of preparatory and qualification modules. These would contain material required for access to particular occupational fields, or to specific training or educational opportunities, which the pupil hoped to pursue later; and the content of these courses, or modules, would have been agreed with the specific educational or occupational organizations.

Such job-specific and 'higher education-specific' courses would be offered in conjunction with a programme of more general courses related to work. Work experience and practical, pre-training workshop courses might take place in outside industrial locations; or they might be located in industrial units on the campus. A model for such units can be found in industrial therapy units in psychiatric hospitals. They aim to smooth the passage to the outside world by enabling the patient to experience a controlled version of outside reality. Recurrent education institutions would have the responsibility of easing their pupils into the future in a similar way.

In addition, the institution would be the local agent for the diversity of academic, and other, courses made available by distance learning methods. It would have to operate all its courses in a flexible way which ensured that every option was available when and where it was needed, and not confined to those who could attend the centre on a full-time basis. Every course would be open to part-time students and to adults, who would be learning alongside children. Adults might be using courses to develop a new occupational route in their life, or to follow a temporary interest unconnected with work. Whatever purpose they had in mind, an educational programme could be devised for them. For example, an arrangement of pre-training, workshop skills, remedial education and work experience might be ideal for a redundant worker with an obsolete skill. Some preparatory modules of academic or work-orientated study might make up into a useful package for a woman returning to work. In a recurrent education institution adults might be taking courses as part-time or full-time students, during the day, evening or weekend, at holiday times, or during working hours as a result of paid educational leave. All options, whether for young people or adults, would be applied in flexible ways.

There would be no place in this kind of organization for the idea of 'nine till four' education. Shift-working, both through the day and through the year, would allow the fullest possible service to be maintained. The teaching in these institutions must be resource-intensive if such a wide range of options were to be available, and the role of teachers would change from narrow subject specialism to broad expertise in teaching and learning. The implications of this change for existing teachers are examined later in this chapter. But an essential task within the organization would be to assemble from the range of learning possibilities available in the institution an individual package for each student, a package which would change as the student progresses and is assessed.

A major feature of a recurrent education system would therefore be the individualization of adolescent education, so that the low-ability, the average and the gifted child could all be taken to their limit within a framework of truly comprehensive education. Accelerated paths to qualifications would be possible. For instance, young people wishing to become medically qualified could add to their core of general education some of the modules which the teaching hospitals would prescribe for their prospective students. Such an accelerated programme of career development would be educationally acceptable because other options were not being permanently closed. The students could return to take other options at a later stage. Throughout the entire educational system the accent would be on individual programming of the available learning opportunities.

The most important feature of the secondary education syllabus would be the explicit separation of qualification objectives from the general education objectives. The attainment of qualifications would be openly asserted as a school function by the schools themselves, and they would be dictating the terms of the qualification process in the interests of each of their pupils. The routes through secondary education would be determined by the aspirations of the individual students, in consultation with their educational guides. It would follow that employers, and institutions of higher education, would have to look more closely at the paths chosen by individual pupils, and not rely on crude grading devices. External examinations, internal learning modules and work experiences, monitored and assessed, would all be possible routes to qualification. The single route to successful qualification, through external examination, would be the exception. This more sophisticated and discriminating approach to the business of qualifying would enable important distinctions to be made between the one task of sifting out those who were equipped for immediate entry to full-time higher education, and the very different task of choosing potentially successful employees. Selection problems would only arise where all applicants for a place in full-time higher education, or a job position, had successfully completed a route to the particular qualifications required, and where no distinctions could legitimately be made between the different paths which each of them had taken.

The selection problem could therefore be considered in isolation from the two functions of basic education and of obtaining qualifications. It would not need to dominate the curriculum of secondary education, as it would no longer be the key to every pupil's future prospects. Nevertheless, the problem of selection would still exist, and needs to be tackled. At present, competing applicants for jobs or for university places are judged by the number and the grades of their examination passes. These provide very simple ways of putting a given age range into a pecking order. But, as we have seen, such yardsticks are less precise and of less predictive value than they appear, quite apart from their damaging effect on the total curriculum of secondary education. More sensitive means of selection, where necessary, would be provided by a mixture of aptitude tests and student profiles, both for jobs and for places in higher education. Aptitude tests provide both relevance and objectivity. Detailed student profiles would incorporate internal and subjective assessments of the various secondary school learning experiences undertaken by the individual concerned. Together, they could provide a sensitive means of selection and a reasonably accurate prediction of future performance. Both are already in use in some institutions. Some employers and some Industrial Training Boards assess potential employees' aptitudes themselves in order to ensure that workers are suited to the work they are taking up. Such employers feel that external examinations and the kind of testing used by schools are simply not sufficiently useful guides.

At present, aptitude testing is insufficient by itself. The process is not sophisticated enough to provide the necessary precision in estimating the relationship between the results of the tests and the requirements of a job. One major problem is caused by the difficulty which employers have in forecasting manpower needs. Since they are unable to predict the type of trained personnel they will need in, say, four years' time, it becomes difficult to establish the particular aptitudes to test for. Some Industrial Training Boards in Britain have encountered this problem in their efforts to devise fair and accurate ways of governing entry into trades. And in the USA the difficulty of achieving a close relationship between test and job requirement has made aptitude testing the subject of a Supreme Court decision. Nowadays an employer in the USA has to show a 'manifest relationship' between test and job to avoid 'unjust' discrimination.[7] But aptitude tests, however much they can be improved, are still a more accurate guide to future scholastic or work performance than the present system of examinations, which is fortunate never to have been legally required to show a 'manifest relationship' with anything worth while at all – it relates only to itself.

Various forms of profile are also being used and are widely accepted as possible alternatives to any single method of assessment. The National Association for Teachers in Further and Higher Education (NATFHE) accepted, in a pamphlet on assessment, that 'in future it may become accepted that the only fair assessment of the student is the profile'.[8] NATFHE believes in the usefulness of recording the performance and attitudes of students over a wide range of skills, knowledge and other personal attributes. Profiles can provide a range of information and a much broader picture of each student than any single set of marks or grades. The Head Teachers' Association of Scotland has recently completed a research project on the value and potential of profiles in conjunction with the Scottish Council for Research in Education.[9] The Association stated: 'We believe that what are increasingly required in the 14 to 16 range of the secondary school are not so much terminal measures of achievement to be used for selection purposes, as kinds of assessment which provide teachers, parents and pupils with guidance.' The project produced a system, similar to that recommended in *The Whole Curriculum 13–16*,[10] which makes possible the recording of information about a pupil's basic skills, achievement in subject areas and personal qualities. At present the temptation is to use such a system with those groups in existing secondary schools who fall outside the ability ranges for GCE or CSE. The RPA (Record of Personal Attainment),[11] which is in use in over seventy secondary schools, and a variant system which stresses experience and not attainment, the RPE (Record of Personal Experience),[12] which is in use in a few schools, are tagged as 'new curriculum activators'. They play the same role for the less able as examinations do for the academic streams. This is, of course, a limitation not inherent in the idea of profiles but imposed by the situations in which they are being used. The Head Teachers' Association of Scotland felt that 'The document should be externally validated and underwritten by appropriately constituted bodies. We [the Association] would see these bodies as offering a comprehensive assessment service which would in time supersede the present system of exams at 16+.'[13]

Dore suggests that aptitude tests and profiles might not be sufficient for all selection processes. A final arbiter, if one were needed to complete a specific selection task, might be general knowledge or intelligence tests, because such tests cannot be prepared for directly. And, in the event of total deadlock, random selection might be necessary.[14] In these ways, selection by society of its cleverest young people – an important and necessary process in itself – would no longer be the major determinant of school syllabuses taken by all young people. This replacement, in the curriculum for young people, of the competitive struggle for certification by a more humane series of goals would imply a similar shift in the ways that adult performance is assessed and graded. In an education system with many routes to self-development which are all considered worth while, assessment must be applied carefully, where and as it is appropriate. Forms of assessment which are crudely and indiscriminately applied throughout the system serve only to create academic hierarchies and a social ladder. An important aim of a recurrent system is the opening up to many more people of traditional, structured routes to qualification and certificates. But it is equally important that the system increases the status of the many other routes to different kinds of personal development. An excessive emphasis on accreditation and certification leads towards the meritocratic state, in which education's intrinsic values are lost, in which, for example, an individual's achievement in acquiring basic educational skills would be denied, because it did not lead to any qualification, and in which the importance of such non-assessable areas as education for leisure, for parenthood, for community involvement and for citizenship would be disregarded.

All these new or different approaches to education in a recurrent system have implications for existing teachers, and these implied changes in the role of teachers all stem from the new, raised level of aggregation at which institutions would be operating. Not only would most specialist teachers be expected to make their skills available to students of all ages, but many would also have to display new kinds of educational skills altogether. Teachers will have to become experts in the teaching/learning process, not so much having knowledge of any one particular subject, as having the ability to lead their pupils and students to knowledge and understanding. Their role will be that of a guide taking students through course material, some of which they produce and some of which is produced for them. They might have very little face-to-face contact with students at all, spending most of their time producing materials for others to use; or they might be devising and monitoring programmes of distance learning.

Class or group teaching would not be the only activity of value, or even the basic framework of the educational process. It would be only one of many possible teaching/learning strategies within an institution. As the range of options on offer increases, and a much more individualized system of resource-based learning emerges, the possibility and usefulness of group teaching in a classroom may diminish. Young pupils will no longer necessarily be advancing through the institution in arbitrary year groupings. The fixed time patterns of the school day would have to lose their rigidity. Teachers might have to travel to their students outside the institution. Their time-table might include evening and holiday work, in order to accommodate part-time or correspondence students. These are some of the implications of flexibility, and of looking at education with a raised perspective. In a recurrent system they would be the norm.

Even more crucial to the success of recurrent education than this flexible approach to teaching will be the creation of sophisticated teams of educational counsellors. Guidance and counselling will be needed early in everyone's educational career. Both work and academic explorations of adolescence would be individually tailored, with the targets for each pupil subject to regular reassessment. If the least able, as well as the most gifted, are to be encouraged to take their learning to its limits at any one time, they especially will need to have confidence in their counsellors. In an individualized system of educational opportunities it will be the counselling service which ensures that the system is genuinely comprehensive. Guidance and counselling on a vast scale will also be the glue which cements together the manpower and the manhood goals of a recurrent education system. The counselling service will be central to all branches of education. Another professional skill needed in education will be the ability to liaise with industry and with social organizations of all kinds. The educator as impressario, as course compiler, as guide, as counsellor and as link man – these will be the new specialisms in a recurrent system. To some extent all of them can be built on to existing jobs. In schools today there are already technical and resource assistants, counsellors and careers officers. They need to be brought from the fringe of the school system to its centre, and to be endowed with the same professional status and rewards as the face-to-face teacher. They are potentially the central cogs of recurrent education.

Ultimately the flexibility of the recurrent system will rely on those one step away from the teaching and learning process, on the administrators, planners and enablers who will structure educational provision and programmes, who will tailor staff and resources to meet learning needs and who will co-ordinate the work of the institution. The role of these specialists cannot be so easily extrapolated from existing practices. But recurrent education will depend on creative administration by educational co-ordinators who see their task, and challenge, as the development of educational solutions to changing problems. These administrators will have responsibility for devising the broad strategies of their institutions. They will be the interpreters of the demands placed on the education system, and the directors of the educational search for latent or unexpressed needs. They will be able to communicate to the various specialists who can provide the tools needed to initiate educational strategies and solutions. But they themselves will not be specialists in the traditional sense. Rather, they will be educational brokers, harnessing not only professional educators but the whole range of informal educative institutions – firms, libraries, museums, local media, significant organizations of all kinds – to the needs of individuals and groups. In themselves such administrators would, in Schon's phrase, 'raise the level of aggregation' at which educational problems were considered. They would be able to react quickly to new situations because they would perceive the education system itself as a means of helping people come to terms with new situations. Their professional interest and identity would not be invested in any specific aspect of the status quo, but rather in their ability to make it change where necessary without too much disruption or suffering.

All these changes in the patterns of educational work would only emerge as a consequence of new forms of training, not so much 'teacher-training' as 'educator-training'. The successful performance of a recurrent system would depend on the quality of such training, both the induction courses preparing people to work in flexible educational organizations, and the in-service training which would develop the skill armoury of the staff as it was needed. A training function could be built on to each institution on a modular basis, with outside expertise called in where necessary. In every institution a recurrent education programme of staff training would be operating alongside the public recurrent education programmes.

The local, comprehensive, all-age institutions of the recurrent education service would be its front line, and its main access point for most people, first as children and later as adults. The most obvious feature of such institutions would be the preparatory and exploratory activities of adolescent education which they would contain. But after their compulsory education in these local institutions, individuals would at some time move into the sector of post-school opportunities, and frequently into more specialized provision than the local education centres could provide. For this extended adult sector to work effectively at local, regional and national levels, it would have to display four characteristics. Diversity, accessibility, transferability and accountability are the essential ingredients of a truly comprehensive system of education. It is impossible to conceive of comprehensive education in Britain until adults are included naturally, and as of right. But adults, far more than children, will expect to have choice, to be given incentives, to feel a sense of progression and to take a degree of control over their educational activities.

Diversity is the foundation. Opportunities for education during adulthood need to be as diverse as can be devised. The automatic association of adult education with leisure or recreation must be abandoned. Adulthood is itself a long period of personal development, longer than and at least as important as development in the adolescent period. It is a time of shifting orientations punctuated by dramatic events such as marriage, job changes, the birth of children, the retirement and death of family members. Whether to cope with new work roles, with family responsibilities, with aspirations to take part in politics and civic life, with new leisure opportunities, or with any changing situation whatsoever, recurrent education envisages that individuals will find it useful to step into a student role. There would be diversity of provision for adults at all points in a curriculum scale, from basic communication skills to advanced research. Opportunities would exist at every level for part-time as well as full-time study, for resource-based, individualized learning as well as learning in groups, and for both long-term and short-term study programmes.

Accessibility is equally vital in order to ensure a mass system. The opportunities for adults to learn must be genuinely open to every member of society, without any financial strings or other disincentives. For at least a generation one imagines the necessity to use forms of positive discrimination to encourage people who have most cause to reject education to take up their rightful opportunities. Paid educational leave is the most important measure to promote accessibility to educational opportunity. Alone, however, it will not be sufficient. The Venables Report on Continuing Education[15] pointed out the large numbers of adults who are not in employment – women at home, the unemployed and the retired – who will also need to have access to education made easier for them.

Accessibility to adult education means that people will

be enabled to take courses of their choice at recurring intervals. This implies that these courses will be available when
and where the student can use them. A considerable increase
in the use of distance learning methods can be envisaged,
therefore, in a system of recurrent education. If correspondence courses are to become an easy and natural path to
educational experience, they will require, as the Open
University has displayed, extensive use of skilful counselling
and guidance techniques. Adult education, especially in its
vocational guises, still retains an aura reminiscent of Charles
Darwin and Samuel Smiles combined. In past years only
the fittest could survive the bleak hours of 'night school'
and self-improvement. Such images are inappropriate to
mass education. The Open University has shown that a mixture of well-designed individual study, occasional and inten-
sive group work and long-term counselling can function
very satisfactorily at degree level. All types of education
could benefit from this mixture.

Alongside a diversity of educational opportunities and
accessibility to them must be incorporated the notion of
transferability. There can be no dead-ends in a recurrent
education system. Failure would always be temporary and
never irrevocable. The Ontario Report on post-secondary
education in 1972 emphasized the need for ever open doors
at all educational levels:

> We are convinced that even if wide accessibility and even
> diversity were achieved, our purpose would be defeated if
> there were insufficient opportunities from institution to
> institution, from programme to programme, from profession
> to profession. We are, therefore, offering recommendations
> designed to . . . provide orderly procedures for transfers of
> abilities, aptitudes and skills (not just formal credits) from
> one post-secondary enterprise to another, and, indeed, from
> any relevant activity in one's life to the educational pro-
> cess.[16]

In a recurrent system accreditation from childhood, or the

lack of it, would be neither a passport nor a barrier to entry into adult education. Entry requirements would be based quite simply on the ability of students to take the course offered. Their success or failure on previous courses would be one guide to their ability, but not necessarily the most important criterion. One aspect of transferability is the acceptance of other countries' academic qualifications. The equivalence of British qualifications with those of EEC countries is an important factor in establishing free job movement alongside free trade. But transferability applies with equal force within each country. The barriers are just as strong internally as they are internationally. Transfer from one job to another and from one profession to another will need to become an easy and natural career progression, instead of a difficult hurdle and with the cost of a painful personal adjustment.

A fourth ingredient of recurrent education is *accountability*. It is not an absolute essential in the same way as the the other three. Recurrent education could exist without any attempt to make it accountable to those paying for it and to those taking part in it, but this is not the case in any country which espouses British political principles. Assertions of accountability in education circles are frequently regarded as attacks on academic liberty, an attempt by philistines and populist politicians to devalue education in general, and to push universities, in particular, into a straitjacket of bureaucratic controls. Accountability in this context, however, is simply an assertion of faith in democratic institutions, and in a democratic pluralism which has traditionally protected the rights of all the individuals and all the minorities which make up mass society. The danger to academic liberty and independence of thought lies, as ever, in the rise of undemocratic political movements, not in the reasonable claim that all providers of public education should be able to justify their provision and the expenditure on it. In practice, accountability in recurrent education would be reflected in two important areas of the system – the way decisions were

taken about policy and expenditure, and the way individual
students were treated.

In 1977 the Taylor Committee recommended much more
representative governing bodies as one answer to the problems of secondary schools.[17] This particular straw in the
wind was received with hostility by professional teachers.
But a greater degree of public involvement, such as that
envisaged in the Taylor recommendations, is the democratic
platform of a recurrent education system. It would become
part of the 'professionalism' of teachers and educators that
they could work effectively with other members of the community. At every level of the education system, and above
all at the level of local institutions, management decisions
about education provision would be taken by representative
bodies, which might be expected to include a number of
consumers, as well as politicians, employers, union officials
and other interested parties. (The current slogan of 'parent
power' would have much less meaning in a recurrent system,
and might be substituted by the more useful notions of
'parent education' and 'parent participation'.)

Equally important is accountability to individual students.
The individually prescribed educational programmes in a
mature recurrent system will require a much greater degree
of accountability on the part of providers. The present
situation, familiar throughout post-compulsory education,
whereby staff salaries can depend on achieving set numbers
of students, can only exist because institutions do not regard
themselves as directly accountable to each of their students.
To suggest a particular course or study option should in no
way be linked to financial recompense or the dictates of an
organization's time-table. Fragnière invents a hypothetical
snapshot of the year 2002 to suggest that there might even
be legal recourse for students who receive shoddy advice
about their educational opportunities:

The Dumuroz family had entered a civil action and claimed
damages of 36,500 European crowns for professional negli-

gence on the part of the Counselling Service of the College of Ouchy-Beau-Rivage in Lausanne. Their mistake had led the young student to waste two years at the University of Vevey, in studies totally unsuited to his aptitudes.[18]

The implications of this seemingly far-fetched proposal are more important than its accuracy as a prediction. In a recurrent education system professionals in all branches of education will have to develop a more conscious and explicit notion of service to their student clients, and the specialist counselling services will be required to have no vested interest in any particular institution or educational organization.

Armed with a belief in these four concepts of wide diversity, open access, easy transfer and public accountability, educational policy-makers would be in a position to create a flexible system. An extensive network of national and regional opportunities would be required to supplement the local, comprehensive, all-age institutions. The structural relationships between national, regional and local levels might not be very different from those existing today, except for a greater amount of devolution. Central government would establish broad policies and statutory priorities. Within that framework regional authorities would have the power to create local policy, and the responsibility for co-ordinating opportunities in an area, in order to ensure no unnecessary duplication. At the level of local institutions there would continue to be a high degree of autonomy so that local decisions on education could be taken and put into effect quickly. But it must be emphasized that this autonomy would be inherent in the institution itself and in its management body, rather than in the person of its chief officer or head teacher. The creation of flexible institutions must involve more devolution away from central authority to those regional or local decision-makers who are in a position to react quickly to new challenges. At all three levels the management of recurrent education would draw together the learning programmes which are at present separately controlled by the Department of Education and Science, local education authorities and schools on the one hand, and the Department of Employment, the Industrial Training Boards, the Manpower Services Commission and the private training schemes on the other.

If institutions are to symbolize the flexible, adaptable personality which they have been set up to help create, they will need to be capable of changing themselves from within. This even has architectural implications. It will be much easier for institutions to shed old functions and develop new activities if educational buildings themselves have been designed for quick change and easy adaptability. This need has already been recognized in some industrial premises which can be converted from factory to office space and back again as required, and at minimum cost and inconvenience. Such flexible buildings – 'long-life, loose-fit, low-energy' – are composed of units which are in themselves both divisible and extendable. Moreover, separate units can be added on, or 'plugged in', to the central establishment, as a cheap way of coping with increased activities or numbers, and they can be removed again as the situation changes. In this way the very architecture would symbolize the functions of recurrent education.

The type of recurrent education system envisaged in this chapter could not be created in one fell swoop by administrative or legislative decree. No reform will ever be the *final* reform. Just as the modes of teaching and learning styles and of institutional behaviour will reflect the nature and aims of the system, so the way in which recurrent education is brought into existence will colour people's attitudes to it and its performance. Administrative and legislative decisions cannot create openness; they cannot bring about the desire to reinterpret educational goals, or to forge new and unexpected links in educational networks. The crucial task of helping people to recognize and use the possibilities of the system will be faced continuously at all levels. Administrative and legislative recognition will be necessary to regularize practice. But it must not be allowed to fossilize only one pattern of activity. The permanent values of a recurrent system will not emerge from any one piece of legislation, however enlightened and all-embracing it may appear; they will emerge from new processes and new attitudes spread throughout society. The statute book, no less than every institution's educational programmes, will need constant revision to keep in line with social change.

References

1 B. Schwarz, in *Permanent Education* (A Compendium of Studies), Strasbourg, Council of Europe, 1970, pp. 103ff.

2 I. Lister, *Deschooling: A Reader*, Cambridge University Press, 1974, p. 11.

3 Quoted in J. Barbash, *Work in a Changing Industrial Society. Final Report on Conference*, Paris, OECD, 1975, p. 28.

4 PEL Project Director, J. Killeen, Middlesex Polytechnic, Capel House, Bullsmore Lane, Waltham Cross, Hertfordshire. Report due 1979–80.

5 G. Fragnière, (ed.) *Education Without Frontiers*, London, Duckworth, 1976, pp. 111ff.

6 Bloom *et al.*, *A Taxonomy* (see note 12 to Chapter 4).

7 US Supreme Court, 8 March 1971: Griggs *v.* Duke Power Co.

8 National Association of Teachers in Further and Higher Education, *Assessment*, London, 1977.

9 Scottish Council for Research in Education, *Pupils in Profile*, London, Hodder & Stoughton, 1977.

10 Schools Council Working Party on the Whole Curriculum, *13–16: The Report of the Schools Council Working Party on the Whole Curriculum 1971–74*, Working Paper 53, London, Methuen, 1975.

11 'RPA' – Account, in *The Times Educational Supplement,*

128   Education and the Challenge of Change

1 April, 1977. (Based at Swindon Curriculum Development Centre.)

12   *RPE – The Development of a New Curriculum Activator in Secondary Schools*, South Brent, Devon, RPE Publications, 1975.

13   Scottish Council for Research in Education, *Pupils in Profile*, p. 28 (see note 9 above).

14   Dore, *The Diploma Disease*, pp. 153–62 (see note 6 to Chapter 1).

15   The Open University, *Report of the Committee on Continuing Education* (The Venables Report), December 1976, p. 28.

16   Quoted in Burgess, *Education after School*, pp. 240–2 (see note 24 to Chapter 5).

17   *A New Partnership for our Schools* (see note 26 to Chapter 4).

18   Fragnière (ed.), *Education Without Frontiers*, p. 82 (see note 5 above).

Chapter 7

The Way Ahead: the Front-Line Institutions

In considering the practical creation of a system of recurrent education, the most difficult set of institutions to visualize is the front-line, the local centres which will be both providers of courses and access points to the system as a whole. These local centres will need to be an integral part of the neighbourhood in which they operate. They must symbolize the possibilities of the entire system and be open to the whole age range. Equally, they must have a wide knowledge of the entire system and be able to offer a range of information and counselling services, directing people where necessary to other institutions or modes of learning which can offer more specialized educational services. The provision offered within the institutions themselves will be appropriate to their locality. It will therefore be adapted as often as is necessary to suit the changing requirements of its local clients. Such front-line institutions of recurrent education will have close contacts with other agencies in the locality, not just with its other, specialist educational providers, but also with its major economic and political organizations and its social and recreational outlets. These local bases will be engaged in a constant process of looking for, as well as responding to, educational possibilities in their neighbourhood. They will be the educational service stations of the future.

We would suggest that there are growth points in our present education system which could be developed to create an effective front-line network of this kind. On the one hand,

the colleges of further education, particularly those that
have developed 'tertiary' functions, are clearly well equipped
to develop in this direction. They are flexible; they see their
work against a 'service' background and they are beginning
to break down artificial age barriers, seeing their objectives
in terms of all those aged 16 and over. But colleges of
further education are too thinly scattered. These colleges
alone could not form the basis of a network which provides
easy, local access points to a recurrent system. If we look
for institutions well provided with facilities and relatively
widely spread across the country, we must consider, although
possibly reluctantly, the secondary or area comprehensive
school. For reasons already noted, existing secondary schools
tend to be preoccupied with their own goals and are too
inward-looking to handle easily the openness and flexibility
of approach which must characterize recurrent education.
They see education in terms of teaching children aged 11 to
16, or 11 to 18. But, despite these strong objections, there is
one powerful and positive argument for the secondary school
as the key growth point for recurrent education. It cannot
be repeated too often that recurrent education is not adult
education writ large. A diverse and flexible array of educational opportunities for those over the age of 16, however
great the need and attractive the presentation, will fail to
offer a mass education service if large numbers of the
potential students continue to be given a lifelong distrust of
education as a result of their secondary school experiences.
For recurrent education to succeed, it is essential that the
education offered to 11 to 18-year-olds is modified, and an
institution based on existing secondary schools would be in
a position to transform the attitudes of pupils towards education at an early and important stage of their lives.

There is also a geographical advantage to secondary
schools. In rural areas especially, further education colleges
are too far apart. Secondary schools are geographically
spread in a pattern which guarantees reasonable access to
most people. Frequently they have their own transport net-

works. Primary schools, which might be thought even more local and convenient, will usually be too small for the large-scale extended use envisaged in a recurrent system.

Even in cities and large towns, where it is considered more practicable to convert further education colleges or tertiary colleges into the front-line institutions of recurrent education, it would still be advisable for secondary schools to be closely involved and widely used in the system. In a recurrent system no educational institution should be able to carry on its activities in more or less total ignorance of the work of other educational institutions, as they do today. The urban secondary school may not become the major provider of extended education, but it could at least act as an information and counselling centre, and as an out-station for specific day and evening courses. In these ways it would recognize some responsibility for the education of adults as well as of children in its area; and it is only by creating this link between secondary education and the system's wider opportunities, in the minds of the providers of education, as well as of consumers, that recurrent education will become meaningful to them, and hence real to everyone.

If the area comprehensive secondary school is to be adapted to this new role of an educational service station in a recurrent system, whether as main local provider or as an out-station of another centre, it will need to add on many functions. This is not as unlikely a development as it may appear. For a variety of reasons, many secondary schools are already taking steps which point the way towards these changes in educational attitudes. They are becoming more outward-looking. For instance, most local authorities, if not as yet most head teachers, accept the desirability of using school premises for more than just a day school. Educational plant can often be the only community facility in an area and people are beginning to expect its wider use. For a long time adult education classes, of the usual restricted non-vocational kind, youth clubs and adult groups, have found an evening meeting-place in secondary schools up and down the country. In recent years many schools have moved closer to their local community through community work and work-experience schemes. These schemes have involved links with local social workers and employers, though, as we have noted, such attempts to provide more realistic educational experiences are usually confined to the less academically able, or 'difficult', children.

Whether it embraces outside interests or has them forced on it, secondary education can no longer ignore the locality in which it operates. More and more secondary schools feel the pressure to explain their role to parents, employers and the general public. The rise of parent–teacher associations has led many schools to the recognition that there are tangible financial benefits to be gained by close contacts with parents. But they have to recognize obligations as well, and in 1977 the Taylor Report crystallized these in connection with school governing bodies.

Opening up secondary education institutions can be managed in various ways. At one organizational extreme is the school which permits other agencies in as fee-paying tenants and has no other expectations of the relationship. At the other extreme is the joint management scheme covering all users of the institution and making no advance assumptions about priorities. The more committed a school becomes to the idea of widening its activities and encouraging joint use, the greater become its management problems. School staff accustomed to having premises available to them may find they have to book 'their' rooms a long way ahead. The school may find 'its' sports facilities unavailable at certain times of the day or at weekends. Procedures have to be devised to ensure that the tenants or joint users have full access to the equipment of the institution. Such changes do not come easily, and require adjustments of attitude at all levels of the school, from caretakers to governors.

Despite these problems some large joint-use centres have been established successfully. The Rowlinson Centre in Sheffield incorporates a 2,000-pupil school, with 250 in the sixth form, an adult education centre with 3,000 students, a youth club with over 1,000 members and a busy sports centre. Priorities for expenditure are decided by a management team, which is faced with the added complication that the District Council provides one set of finance for recreation and leisure, while the County Council provides resources for education and youth work. This centre provides a useful model for one form of educational development in urban areas. Much more common than urban campuses of the Rowlinson model are smaller-scale institutions in some rural and suburban areas, known variously as village colleges, community colleges, or, simply, community schools. A number of local authorities in all parts of Britain are developing the notion of 'community education' in these institutions which, like the Rowlinson Centre, incorporate secondary school, adult education, youth work and the public use of premises.

As with so many terms used in educational discussion, the phrase 'community education' can cause confusion. Many people connect it with the experimental developments in the educational priority area (EPA) schemes in London, Liverpool and elsewhere. This kind of urban community education has been described by Eric Midwinter and is very much concerned to provide remedial or 'second-chance' education for those who are thought to need it most.[1] In our view it would be unfortunate if the mass potential of community education, as a continuing first chance for everyone, was lost sight of because of its close association with areas of most severe challenge and obvious need.

Village and community colleges provide working examples of community education which are useful in considering a national framework or network of front-line recurrent education institutions. Unlike the very large urban campuses, these rural or small-town institutions tend to serve a limited geographical area and a more easily definable population, though not necessarily a more homogeneous community in any strict sociological sense. Underlying the development of the community education theme is a belief that by integrating the separate components of an institution the whole will become greater than the sum of the parts. By tying together the secondary school, the adult education centre, informal youth provision and the community users, the activities of each of these four aspects will be enriched. School performance is improved by closer associations with its neighbourhood. The adult education programme is enhanced by the easy availability of qualified school staff and the superior facilities of a school. Young people and the other users are enabled by the proximity of their activities to see one another in mutually comprehending ways and as potential sources of help. Groups using the premises, in all kinds of clubs or societies, are able to set their own specific activities in the wider context of a community institution, and to make contributions to the general good as well as to their own members. The processes which allow the whole institution to represent more than the sum of its parts on this day-to-day basis also allow it to innovate, and to develop activities, to an extent which lies beyond the scope of any one of its components. Potentially, the school, the adult sector, the youth sector and the affiliated groups can each call on the others to ensure that the educational, recreational and leisure provision in the neighbourhood is as full and as appropriate as possible.

Community colleges can be seen as important forerunners and foundation stones of a recurrent system in Britain. They represent the major attempt so far to introduce a flexible education service able to cope with change. Community education is nevertheless frequently criticized. As a concept it is imprecise, and as an activity it seems frequently to have promised more than it has in fact delivered. But it provides a seed and a pointer to the future by displaying, virtually alone among established forms of education in Britain, the lifelong and life-wide perspectives which must characterize a recurrent education system. Community education provides a model to show how the front-line institutions of a mass, comprehensive local education service might come into being. It is not the specific achievements or innovations of community colleges which constitute their claim to be regarded as focal points of future development. This claim rests much more on their processes of operating and of decision-making, processes which are marked by three key characteristics – service, partnership and flexibility.

Community education is set firmly within the *service* tradition of education, and this is one reason why it is not always easy to graft community education on to secondary schools, which have tended to perceive themselves as autonomous rather than servicing institutions. But perceptions can be changed, as the example of adult education in Britain testifies. In the 1950s many professional adult educators found unacceptable the view of adult education as a general service to any adult who cared to make use of it. They preferred to see adult education as a 'movement' helping the uninitiated towards an appreciation of the civilizing values of the 'great traditions'.[2] The internal virtues of the subject disciplines were stressed much more than any utilitarian or non-academic requirements of most potential adult students. Today, however, adult education is everywhere understood as an undifferentiated service incorporating all levels of learning, and with some potential for all adults. It is no longer a ladder for the few, but a service for the many.

Community education takes this service perspective as its starting-point. There is no provision hallowed by tradition, nothing which must continue because someone was appointed to teach it. The criterion for all educational activity is that people require it. The curriculum development movement in conventional education has required the same kind of transformation in institutional attitudes, a turning away from simply providing a traditional or customary range of educational experiences. Like community education, the curriculum development movement depends on the definition of needs and the design of appropriate strategies. The priorities of an institution can no longer be assumed; they have to be discussed. Community education institutions expect to be open and innovative rather than exclusive and resistant to change, and professionals in community education do not expect to limit their activity to a specific set of tasks for which they feel themselves trained. On the contrary, both institutions and professionals have their roles defined to a large extent by the people they are serving, and one of their major functions is to help with this definition which will obviously change from year to year and client to client.

Once an educational institution is imbued with this service approach, the notion of *partnership* with the students and with the community at large becomes the essential mode of operation. It becomes impossible for the professional educator to draw up educational programmes without reference to the students they aim to attract. The role of the institution has to be closely connected with the roles of other services in the community if the education service is to respond to its community sensitively and in appropriate ways. In some institutions this idea of a partnership with the community is symbolized by the concentration of several such services on the same site. In some Cambridgeshire village colleges, and elsewhere, the existence of libraries, health centres, leisure centres, sports centres, play centres and even shopping centres, operating alongside the school, adult education and youth provision, helps to create a partnership between the formal education sector and what Schwarz calls the 'parallel school' of all the educative agencies found in any community.[3] Even without such physical proximity, community education departments will see one of their tasks as the forging of links with all the important agencies and organizations in the community.

External partnership of this kind enables the institution not only to understand the community which it is set up to serve but also to tap the educational resources of the community itself. The wide range of 'partners' which a community education service can develop in industry or public administration, in shops or health centres, in voluntary organizations or statutory social services, becomes not only a source of potential students and new educational programmes, but also a pool of teaching, and sometimes financial, resources. A sensitive analysis of the educational needs in any given community is only possible within this framework of partnership. Frequently such analysis will lead to traditional programmes of adult education, among other things, but not necessarily so. This kind of partnership is also the necessary background to any successful innovation. The development of new educational projects becomes an interactive process in which a professional works with potential students before any course or activity is given its final shape. In every social field successful innovation depends on careful preparation, on what has been called 'the cultivation of the host culture'.[4] The variety of strategies in community education stems from potential partnerships with every conceivable aspect of the host culture. The community and its education centre can eventually become locked together in a process of organic growth, each taking strength from the other.

Internal partnerships with students and users of educational institutions are as important as outside partnerships. A factor uniting all institutions of community education is the theme of participatory management. Decisions about education policy and specific provision are taken by a team consisting of people who are actual or potential consumers of the community education service in partnership with the day-to-day professional staff. Some institutions have incorporated this notion of power-sharing with the community more effectively than others. The statutory requirements and legal obligations which are placed upon secondary school head teachers do not at present always encourage the creation of such democratic partnerships. Where a community school does have an active management committee drawn from its users, it is not always able to work in harmony alongside the more traditional authority of the school governors. But the process of participatory management cannot be regarded as an optional extra in community education. The decision-making process is at the heart of community education. Participation is both an educational goal in itself and a means of achieving a programme of opportunities which will match educational needs within a geographical area. Any attempt to describe or evaluate community education must understand the importance of this participatory process, which can and must lead institutions to develop a wide variety of activities. Just as one cannot understand a disease by merely looking at its separate symptoms, without considering such potential unifying factors as blood circulation or bacteria, so one cannot understand community education by simply cataloguing its external manifestations or class programmes. The working of a community education institution can only be judged by reference to the particular area in which it operates. The Devon County Council Working Party Report on community colleges emphasized the individuality expected of each institution: 'The purpose of a community college is to reflect the interests and serve the needs of the community in which it is situated. An essential quality is that it is local and therefore individual. There can be no exact blueprint.'[5]

Partnership with the community in the management of institutions has been shown to work not only in the more successful community colleges but in a considerable number of adult education institutions. In particular, the Workers' Educational Association and the Educational Centres' Association have both insisted on the importance of flourishing participation by their student members. Nevertheless, it is easy in all forms of education for policy-makers at national and regional level, and for professional staff themselves, to pay lip service to notions of partnership and participation. Integral to a future survice of mass education, administered in local institutions, is the willingness to devolve a real measure of decision-making power to the local institutions themselves. This autonomy would belong not to the professional staff but to the participatory structure of management. Educating the managers would then become a continuing activity no less than the in-service education of the professionals. And all those concerned with making and implementing policy decisions would need to understand the notion and practice of administrative flexibility, which is the third key characteristic of community education.

The concepts of service and partnership in community education are intimately linked with this concept of *flexibility*. Henry Morris, in his 1925 memorandum on village colleges, saw clearly that the kind of institution he was proposing would have an inherent flexibility that would enable it to survive: 'The Village College would not outlive its function for the main reason that it would not be committed to any intellectual or social dogma or to any sectional point of view. Intellectually it might be one of the freest of our English institutions.'[6] Perhaps he underestimated the inflexibility which will continue to exist in any education system that is dominated by the education of children and young people. Community education is the starting-point for a more rational view, because it alone treats everyone in a given area as a potential recipient of its services. Only by bringing into focus all the educational arrangements for a defined geographical area, from pre-school to post-retirement opportunities, is it possible to create a flexible operation. By seeing the imbalance of the present child-based education system, the possibilities of a future lifelong system become more apparent. The achievement of Henry Morris, and that of the various forms of community education which have followed him, is to provide the vantage-point. The practical reality is still to come. Yet in certain precise ways the community education institutions which already exist do offer a model for future recurrent education institutions. They demonstrate the effectiveness of an institution which operates as a partnership. They show how a programme of educational opportunities and activities can be derived in response to, and as a result of, a participatory analysis of local needs. They display the shift from the centre/periphery model of decision-making, in which decisions taken at the centre are fed out to the grass roots for action, towards the network model, where, as Tom Lovett puts it, 'the needs and interests are defined by those involved in the learning process'.[7] But most of all they represent the nearest approach in the whole education system to a genuinely flexible institution.

Donald Schon shows how flexible institutions have been created in other fields. Two of his models, already mentioned, can be applied to education in general, and community education in particular. He assumes that throughout society there is a requirement for institutions which can adapt, which can themselves learn in order to cope with changes around them. From his examination of industrial concerns faced with the changing expectations of the market-place, Schon showed that successful adaptation depended in part on 'raising the level of aggregation'.[8] By raising their perspectives industrial organizations are enabled to develop a much wider range of strategies, and are therefore less likely to be caught out by short-term changes of fashion or customer preference. The principle can be applied to educational strategy and goals.

If the general goal of secondary education is to educate all the children of a given age range, say 11 to 16-year-olds, the introduction of comprehensive schools can be said to have represented a raising of the level of aggregation in comparison with the bipartite system of the 1944 Education Act. The latter assumed that two lots of horses could be chosen for two separate courses at the age of 11. It precluded any flexibility in secondary education. But the introduction of comprehensive education was only a minor improvement. Flexibility which is confined to secondary education is still not sufficient to achieve the goals of education in the circumstances of the modern world. The comprehensive school does not raise the level of aggregation enough. By developing a community education function on top of the secondary education function, the view is broadened yet again. Flexibility becomes possible by converting the institution into a provider of educational services for all members of a geographical area, irrespective of age, aptitude or previous achievement. The goal becomes education of all kinds for any person, not education of a pre-determined kind for one age range. Operating in this way the institution can be pre-adapted to change. It learns to expect change.

Another of Schon's models for flexible structures is called the 'constellation firm',[9] an image which applies to many of the largest firms, including multinational corporations. As we have seen, a holding company lies at the centre of the firmament of such organizations. This central holding company sets broad policies for the firm, but remains unaffected by the inevitable process of growth and decline among its various subsidiaries and satellite creations. Because it expects such changes, the holding company is equipped to survive them and even to control them. On a much smaller scale, and with very different goals, these constellation firms have their analogues in the management bodies (or committees) of community schools or colleges. These committees can create their own kind of subsidiaries in the form of new courses, new groups or new activities, as new demands or needs are brought to their attention. Decisions are taken, priorities established and resources allocated for the kind of educational services appropriate to the neighbourhood. But at any time these decisions can be reconsidered, priorities questioned and resources redirected, if local circumstances have changed. As courses, groups or activities lose their purpose they can be wound up without any loss of continuity or sense of failure on the part of the management body. Such changes are expected, and the institution's management therefore knows that it must be flexible.

These kinds of institutions are already demonstrating the shift in emphasis which we have suggested must take place in the value given to different types of activity. Community Colleges do not, of course, have any overtly vocational training role at present, and this limits the extent to which they can provide a truly unifying set of experiences. They are, however, with this limitation, offering many routes to continuing self-development. A variety of opportunities to develop role versatility all operate under the college umbrella. Such institutions provide access, in varying ways, to the conventional educational channels, either for qualification or for personal enjoyment; but they are also the brokers for a wide range of other engagements in partnership with voluntary and supported organizations. Bringing people together is at the heart of community education. This constellation of groups around the nucleus of the college provides a range of ways of participating and, for many people, leading, organizing or simply participating in such groups is a route to self-development. Community education can be seen as a bridge carrying educational traffic in two directions. It is easy to see educational institutions as providers of a service *to* a community; but from our point of view it is equally important to see the institution as a means of focusing and harnessing the energy, skills and enthusiasm *of* the community.

The kind of institution outlined above, with its emphasis on service, on partnership and on flexibility, requires a particular kind of professional worker. It is not easy, given the deep-seated myth of stability in society, for any professional to come to terms with a constantly changing pattern of client requirements. But it is the essence of community education, as it will be of a recurrent education system, that what is required will constantly be running ahead of what is being provided. The combination of a service role, the raised perspective and 'constellation' management structures can create institutions in which the whole is truly more than the sum of the parts and in which change is accepted as the norm. Such institutions, however, will stand or fall by the quality of the professionals engaged in the day-to-day implementation of these flexible policies.

Community education requires a body of professional educators who see themselves as brokers as much as providers. They are the linking agents whose work depends on their constant liaison with others, and whose mode of working is in every way collaborative. In devising and constructing educational responses the community education professional must be able to mobilize the skills to be found in the community as well as those of colleagues in specialist educational areas. Ideas of enabling and facilitating are well known in adult education; they suggest that people can be helped to help themselves. The professional in community education embodies the raised educational perspective, and therefore foreshadows the kind of professional generalist who will be needed in a recurrent system – part counsellor, part researcher, part provider and part facilitator.

All this may be scarcely recognizable to those working in community education at present. Community education is hampered everywhere by the low priority given in British education to organizations which are concerned with service rather than with the purveying of traditional academic disciplines. Adult education, defined as being 'non-vocational', can be easily discarded as being of low priority. Government intervention will be required to alter the emphasis of education authorities, and to place community education in its rightful place as the policy shaping the local service stations of a national recurrent education system. But small advances have already been made, despite these difficulties.

In many community schools adults are appearing in school classes, albeit in small numbers.[10] In some colleges staff are being appointed on split contracts: 90 per cent of their time is spent with the day school and the rest is available for work outside. When such appointments become the norm, a *cadre* of community college staff will emerge who should begin to strengthen the ties between the various functions of the college. It brings the concept of shift-working into the day school for the first time. The same colleges are experimenting with block-grant finance. An amount of money is allocated to the college as a whole, to be split between its various functions according to its assessment of local priorities. The path forward for all community colleges depends on the extent to which they can weave the traditionally separated day school, adult education, youth work and community work functions into a whole.

There are some examples of the breakdown of the conventional school day as a result of multi-purpose usage. At Sutton in Ashfield, the Sutton Centre combines a shopping centre, a library, a swimming pool, an ice rink, squash courts, a theatre, a welfare centre and a school. The school day is made up of two blocks, with no bells and no short periods. Adult students work alongside children during the day and the day pupils overlap into evening sessions in a range of courses. Many pupils also work towards CSE Mode 3 examinations with continuous assessment.

It has been necessary to analyse the potential of secondary schools for development as a recurrent education base to show that despite their many inherent disadvantages they possess many positive elements, including the major advantage that such developments will affect the education of children. In many areas the geographical distribution of the secondary school would make it the logical front-line institution, and in rural areas its role would be of paramount importance. Just as secondary schools in the shadow of urban tertiary colleges might be used as referral and counselling bases, so might primary schools in more scattered populations be used similarly.

There is no doubt that the colleges of further education are the most suitable bases for recurrent education in the present climate of educational opinion and attitudes. They are already operating as service institutions; they are used to devising courses appropriate to the needs of local industry. In the same way that community colleges are already beginning, in small ways, to demonstrate the potential of the secondary school base, the new tertiary colleges are showing the potential of the colleges of further education. In fact, similarities exist between the objectives of the community and tertiary colleges. A major objective of Nelson and Colne College, a pioneer of tertiary organization, is the creation of 'a comprehensive programme of post-compulsory educational activities each designed to contribute in some way, however small, to the quality of life of the community'.[11] Such a college provides a range of part-time courses and vocational education for the entire post-16 age group and attempts to generate leisure activities within the community. The tertiary college has the advantage, as a developing recurrent education base, of combining vocational and non-vocational education within the same institution from the beginning; but at the same time, because it can deal only with the products of the compulsory education service, its opportunities to establish the major and widespread changes in attitude which would underlie the provision of a life-long pattern of education are limited. In 1979 there were only fifteen tertiary colleges operating and perhaps their most far-reaching innovation up to date is the development of an embryonic Open College programme. In Lancashire (at Nelson and Colne College) a pattern of course modules is presented which offers a route into higher education other than conventional O and A-levels, as well as one which provides study opportunities that can valuably be followed for their own sake. The courses are followed on a part-time basis with individual tuition and study days. Their successful completion is accepted by Lancaster University and Preston Polytechnic for entry to degree courses, i.e. as the equivalent of two A-levels. These units may be made available through the National Extension College as part of a distance-learning scheme beginning with basic units. Through this project the Nelson and Colne College has helped to establish a large-scale example of distance learning made available through local educational bases. This kind of distance learning must become a key factor in the development of recurrent education institutions.

The seeds, and in some cases the half-grown saplings, which could become our front-line recurrent education bases – the crucial first contact and attitude-developing institutions – are already in existence. Development of the community college and the tertiary college into a network of educational service stations is a real possibility. Both institutions see their roles in terms of tapping local resources and both constantly change in response to needs. The consequent pattern of recurrent education would parallel that which has arisen to satisfy our demands for medical help. Our front-line contact points – the educational equivalent of general practices or health centres – would act as referral centres passing people along to appropriate help at neighbour hood colleges of further education (cottage and district hospitals) and, if necessary, on to other specialist higher education institutions.

References

1   E. Midwinter, *Patterns of Community Education*, London, Ward Lock Educational, 1973.
2   H. L. Wiltshire, 'The Great Tradition in University Adult Education', *Adult Education*, vol. 29, Autumn 1956, pp. 88–97.
3   Schwarz, in *Permanent Education* (see note 1 to Chapter 6).
4   N. J. Georgiades and L. Phillimore, 'The Myth of the Hero-Innovator and Alternative Strategies for Organizational Change', in C. C. Kiernan (ed.), *Behaviour Modification with the Severely Retarded: Study Group of the Institute for Research into Mental and Multiple Handicap*, Amsterdam, Associated Scientific Publications, 1975, p. 313.
5   *Community Colleges in Devon*, Second Working Party Report, Devon County Council, 1970, p. 3.
6   H. Morris, *The Village College Memorandum*, Cambridge University Press, 1925, published as an appendix in H. Rée, *Educator Extraordinary*, p. 155 (see note 12 to Chapter 3).
7   T. Lovett, 'Community Development – A Network

Approach', *Adult Education*, vol. 46, no. 3, September 1973, pp. 157–65.

8 Schon, *Reith Lectures*. See *Beyond the Stable State* (see note 27 to Chapter 3).

9 Ibid.

10 M. Hughes. 'Adult Education on the Cheap: an Extension of Adult Education Provision into the School Classroom', *Adult Education*, vol. 5, no. 4, November 1977, pp. 226–32.

11 *An Introduction to the College,* a paper produced by Nelson and Colne College, Scotland Road, Nelson, Lancashire, p. 2.

Chapter 8

The Way Ahead: Growth Points

Besides community education and tertiary colleges, there are in British education today many other tendencies and institutions from which a recurrent system might grow. Although such growth points do not yet amount to the kind of unified structure or strategy which will eventually signify the arrival of a coherent system, all the examples outlined in this chapter reflect one or more of the key features of a recurrent education strategy as depicted in Chapter 6. They may be only fragments, lacking pattern or co-ordination, and as such they are representative of today's fragmented system; but nevertheless they give cause for optimism. The inevitable incompleteness of the examples in this chapter is also encouraging, because it means that new and forward-looking activity is emerging all the time in various parts of the education and training structures. An overall view of education and training is not yet feasible, but it is possible to find hopeful signs in almost every compartment of the two systems, and to see barriers breaking down either unconsciously, as a result of external pressures, or explicitly, as part of a conscious commitment to the development of recurrent education. The following sections pick out just a few of the organizations and practices which may come to be seen as precursors of a recurrent system, and which illustrate the themes explored throughout this book. Our hope is that the evolution of a recurrent system in Britain will be so rapid that this chapter in particular, and perhaps even the whole book, will very soon appear dated.

School and Pre-school Education

One noticeable feature of British education since the 1960s has been the growth of pre-school education, and in particular of a deprofessionalized playgroup movement run on a largely voluntary basis by parents.[1] There is no more truth in the idea that children under 5 are not ready for education than there is in the similarly old-fashioned idea that adults are too old to learn. Indeed, intellectual growth is so rapid in the first five years of life, and the opportunity so ripe to start developing children's powers of understanding and creativity, that part-time, pre-school education must be an essential preliminary in a total recurrent system. If universal nursery education existed, as recommended by the Plowden Committee in 1967, it might well be possible to delay the entry of children to full-time education until they were 6 or even 7 years old.[2]

The Pre-school Playgroups Association (PPA), which, through its regional organizations, has developed playgroups up and down the country, has also stressed the importance of parental involvement in the education of their children. Not only does this ensure that valuable learning and play techniques are taken back into the home, but also that equally valuable adult education takes place as well. If parenthood is seen as a stage in adult life which is important in its own right, and not just as the means for renewing the species, its educational potential becomes apparent. Many parents begin to acquire the skills and to take on the responsibility necessary for managing playgroups themselves. The PPA's training schemes, often run in conjunction with formal educational institutions, are just as significant, in the context of recurrent education, as its concern for the personal and social development of society's youngest members. Although nursery education, statutory or voluntary, has not yet received sufficient encouragement or resources in Britain, enough has been achieved to show the way ahead.

In the compulsory education sector three trends are especially significant. Like community education, they are all concerned in some way to bring schools closer to the social organizations around them, and to those individuals who are justifiably interested in their work and performance. The Taylor Committee Report in 1977, already mentioned above, was concerned to build accountability in to the structure of schools. It recommended change in both the composition and powers of school governing bodies.[3] More parents and more neighbourhood representatives as governors would help to create the kind of local partnership in education which will render schools less remote and more accountable. Many local education authorities, recognizing the force of the momentum started, or at least boosted, by the Taylor recommendations, have started projects for the in-service education of school governors. One survey in 1978 suggested that 55 per cent of local authorities were in fact already providing, sponsoring or planning to provide some form of training for school governors.[4] But these courses represent only a small step on the path towards full local involvement and effective parental participation in the work of schools. Isolated from any meaningful participation in the formal control of schools, parents tend to pursue choice of school as if it were a fundamental educational issue, almost a human right. But choice of school is of little importance. We have tried to show that in educational terms secondary schools are more significantly marked by their similarity to each other, imposed by the pervasive umbrella of external examinations, than by any superficial differences of curriculum organization and style. The real educational issue is what actually happens in schools, and how it might be improved. The fundamental parental right is not to choose a school, but to attend one!

A second trend growing in importance is the movement to link schools and industry. There are many projects in this field, some initiated by industry, others by educational organizations. Two brief examples must serve to show the potential of them all. Understanding British Industry (UBI) is funded by industry and commerce under the aegis of the Confederation of British Industry. Originally set up in 1966, but redesigned in 1976, 'the objective of the UBI is to help teachers and their pupils to become more aware of the part which industry and commerce play in the social and economic life of our country'.[5] UBI has a large budget, a team of regional officers, and a resource centre in Oxford which provides them with material. It is especially keen to encourage teachers to gain work experience, and to convince companies that they need to be involved with schools, and with teachers, in areas other than simply the recruitment of school-leavers.

The Schools Council Industry Project (SCIP) has grown out of schools rather than out of industry. SCIP, too, has a network of regional officers seeking to establish local links between schools and firms, and to help set up work experience for teachers and pupils. But it is also involved in curriculum change as well.[6] However, UBI, SCIP, and other link schemes are no more than small steps on the path to a full programme of vocational preparation in adolescent education. But they can be seen as a start in the process of breaking down the apartheid which has separated work from education in Britain. The major strand of this process will be the universal provision of paid educational leave for mature students already at work, but to date there has been more serious attention paid to school–work links than to later work–education links.[7]

The third significant development in compulsory education in recent years is also at only a rudimentary stage. This is the move towards a clearer understanding of what happens in schools today, and how schools compare with each other in performance. The Assessment of Performance Unit (APU) was set up by the Department of Education and Science in 1975. Its explicit terms of reference were 'to promote the development of methods of assessing and monitoring the achievement of children at school and to seek to

identify the incidence of under achievement'. But an implication of the APU's work, as of the two developments above,
will be to lead schools and teachers towards a service attitude
both to the individual pupils in their charge and to the community at large. Like school–industry link schemes and like
supporters of the Taylor Committee's proposals, APU has to
expect opposition from within schools. It has to reassure
teachers that a keen interest in what they do is not necessarily
the same as interference in their work, or an attempt to
impose a nationally prescribed curriculum on them. As a
result of its tests, APU hopes to make 'parents, employers
and others better informed about the achievements of
schools', and it also seeks to complement subject-based
assessment with its own forms of assessment, which will give
a 'cross curricular picture of national performance'.[8] This
interesting idea harks back to the early days of examinations,
when it was the school and the form rather than individual
children which were tested by examiners. Since its assessment methods must be applicable to all schools, regardless
of individual differences in their curricula, they may begin
to erode the justification for the external examination system.
APU is the first body which has attempted to look nationally at the performance of schools and to assess them. Its
main results will not appear until the early 1980s, and they
may herald a significant shift away from reliance on external
examinations, towards a better balance of educational opportunities provided in schools.

Further Education and Unified Vocational Preparation

During the 1970s there has been a growing interest and much
development in the education of 16 to 19-year-olds. It is
clear that the learning needs of this age range do not fit
neatly into categories of education and training. Part of the
significance of tertiary colleges is that they provide a structural response to the unification of education and training

opportunities, by combining the traditionally separate functions of sixth-form and technical work in the one institution. The curricular, or content, developments, with the same unifying objectives, are equally significant. One such development gaining in popularity is the notion of unified vocational preparation (UVP).

According to a government statement in March 1976 the essentials of the UVP approach are:

(i) that vocational preparation should be jointly planned and provided by the education and training services, and should combine education and training elements inseparably.

(ii) relevance and realism ... provision should be clearly seen by young people entering work and by employers to be relevant to their needs and should be focused on the working situation.[9]

UVP programmes differ from conventional college courses in two ways that are relevant to recurrent education themes. The organizers, working with colleges and employers, do not design the scheme until they have identified the students and explored with them their individual learning needs: 'There is no doubt that priority must be given to that learning required to make a success of the activities that the individual is presently engaged in.'[10] Second, UVP courses do not lead to external examination or selection: 'UVP caters for a wide range of young workers, helping them with the activities they are already engaged in. Although it might identify and develop unsuspected talents it is not a function of the course to select (for promotion, for instance).'[11] It is also worth noting that a number of UVP courses avoid the use of further education colleges, in order to escape association with an education system to which their young clients feel no attachment and which they may already have shunned.

UVP programmes are aimed at the 40 per cent of school leavers who previously had little or no chance of further education opportunities. But there is no reason why many of the other 60 per cent could not also benefit from the same unified approach to their further education, so that their courses are designed specifically to ease their transition from school to jobs, and not perceived as providing a 'ticket for life'.

There is also continuing pressure for precise vocational preparation in schools. The Engineering Industrial Training Board, pioneers since 1968 of modular training schemes for apprentices, have suggested how a generalized basic engineering training might be introduced into school during the pupil's last two years.[12] Engineering alone is too narrow an approach to work-related education in school; and there is no provision in the Board's proposals for craft training for older students to participate. But at the very least their proposals represent a detailed statement in favour of some form of vocational preparation in schools. Exploration and discovery between the ages of 14 and 16 are still 'more humane and economical than "recovery" classes between the ages of 16 and 18'.[13]

Another development, in both further and higher education, which could be harnessed to the requirements of many more students of all ages in a recurrent system is the flexible course work and modular programmes designed to give a broader educational experience to 16–21-year-olds than is contained in many of the older, established diploma and degree courses. In further education this development of modular course units is largely associated with the Technician Education Council (TEC) and the Business Education Council (BEC). The TEC and the BEC, set up in 1973 and 1974 respectively, are both concerned to work with colleges and further education teachers in order that they can together devise rational and flexible curricula which allow a variety of routes to industrial certificates and diplomas. All their courses are expected to have clearly identified aims and objectives, with assessment procedures that directly relate to these aims and objectives. Although mainly conceived in terms of 'preparing young people' for the complexities of modern life, both the TEC and the BEC recognize the desirability of encouraging more adult students to undertake their courses.[14] And a comprehensive recurrent education strategy would ensure that all programmes and awards in further and higher education were indeed opened up to many more adult students.

A modular approach to further and higher education not only lends itself to the needs of mature, part-time students who have to fit their education into other patterns of work and home life, but also makes easier the possibility of transfer from one course to another, either within an institution or from one institution to another. Such transfer possibilities are essential in a recurrent education strategy. A research project at Exeter University was due to report in 1979 on the present possibilities of transferable educational credits throughout the whole range of further and higher education courses, and on the need for a national information service on such credits.[15] This report may also be a signpost to a future in which university entrance requirements, for example, will take into account courses, and modular units, successfully completed in further education colleges. The basis of transferability, and of diversity, in a recurrent education system will have emerged when almost every full-time course in secondary, further and higher education can be broken down into its constituent parts, or modules, in order that part-time students of any age could take the same course over a longer time period, and perhaps at more than one institution.

Higher Education

In British universities and polytechnics there is a growing body not just of theoretical studies related to concepts like recurrent and continuing education, but also of practical projects, which in a small way exemplify the theories. Although universities, in particular, are generally reluctant to take on an explicit servicing role in their local communities, there has been over the past ten years a noticeable widening in their extra-mural departments of what constitutes 'appropriate university adult education provision'. Many universities and polytechnics are providing education for both sides of industry, education in prisons, and education for many professions and voluntary bodies. A few are closely involved with community projects and various forms of training or 'role education'.[16] In practice, in other words, the traditional distinctions between education and training, vocational and non-vocational, are gradually breaking down even in those institutions which might be most likely to want to retain them. Other developments in one or two higher-education institutions include the use of modular courses, and the use of the principle of credit accumulation, more familiar in North American universities. Oxford Polytechnic offers the opportunity for part-time degree study, or any mixture of full-time and part-time study, through flexible modular courses.[17] The North East London Polytechnic offers a Diploma of Higher Education, based on independent study, and tailors the course to match the needs of students in as precise a fashion as possible. According to Tyrell Burgess, 'the programme differs from others in higher education in that it is based, not upon subject disciplines or upon combinations of subjects, but upon the logic of learning'.[18]

Such developments in higher education, though piecemeal and altogether lacking in co-ordination, might lead in two significant directions. First, all institutions offering higher education in Britain may, sooner or later, see part of their function as the seeking out of potential students of all ages. And they would have to provide, as part of the institution's normal, staple offering, courses of varying lengths, full-time or part-time, especially constructed to meet the particular requirements of such students. A second direction is the parallel development whereby the departments which are to co-ordinate and administer this provision, and this flexible approach to higher education, will take their rightful places in the centre of the institution. Richard Hoggart recommends that:

> The adult or extra-mural or continuing education departments of the universities should in the eighties become much more central within their institutions. Through them . . . the universities could enter an era in which their sense of belonging to their local communities was better fulfilled.[19]

Of all higher education institutions in Britain the Open University is pre-eminent as a growth point for a recurrent system. Its short courses for specific target groups of students provide a particularly valuable model. Not only do its own courses display features like open access, ease of transfer and flexible approaches, but it has also exerted a widespread influence on practices and attitudes in other educational institutions. The 1976 Venables Report on *Continuing Education*, which was widely circulated outside the Open University, contained a number of far-sighted proposals and recommendations in tune with recurrent education, including the setting up of a national advisory service for education, and 'efforts to persuade government to fulfil its undertaking to the International Labour Organization on paid educational leave'.[20] The Open University has initiated many collaborative projects with other agencies in the field of adult education, and will have been a major contributor to the creation of a genuinely comprehensive sector of post-school education, if and when it comes into existence.

Local Authority Adult Education and the Advisory Council for Adult and Continuing Education

We have already noted that 'adult education', as presently understood in Britain, commands few resources and even less esteem. But even within the low-status field of local authority adult education there have developed a number of potentially significant growth points. Several of the best features of adult education came together in the adult literacy scheme, which made a national impact in the mid-1970s.[21]

Once government and public opinion had been alerted to the scale of adult illiteracy in Britain, the success of the scheme depended on the existence of local networks able to respond quickly and effectively when demands were made on them and when central resources were made available. Such networks had in most cases already been built up by adult education organizers. Unlike innovations in other branches of education, it is customary for new adult education courses, projects and priorities to be discussed, decided upon and implemented with considerable speed. Flexibility already exists in this underrated sector of education. The rapid introduction of local adult literacy projects can be compared, for example, with the long-drawn-out introduction of N and F examinations. When and if the latter are finally implemented, they will be yet another example of 'dynamic conservatism', whereby a 'new' solution will be finally applied in about 1990 to problems which were already outdated, and of low priority, in 1980.

Another feature of the adult literacy campaign, related to the flexibility of adult educators and their networks of local contacts, was its use of a large volunteer force, as tutors, resource assistants and administrative helpers. People are the major resource of any education system. To achieve variety and diversity in a recurrent system the skills and expertise of professionals will have to be complemented by the skills and expertise of volunteers. Enlightened nursery, infant and primary school teachers already use volunteer help with young children. The adult literacy campaign showed how volunteers can be used in adult education, and how training programmes can be set up to make the fullest use of their help. As with all the most productive voluntary work, the benefits of using volunteers in education cut both ways. A large number of elderly, home-bound and unem-

ployed people not only have skills to offer but are also
desperately anxious to play a useful role in society. They
respond willingly to requests to place their expertise at other
people's disposal. A number of local 'skill exchange' schemes
have been started along these lines during the 1970s. People
wanting to learn an unusual or specialized skill are put in
touch with anyone who is offering expertise in that area.
An imaginative community education programme might
incorporate such skill exchanges as part of its local education service.[22] One function of recurrent education must be
to ensure that people realize that they have things to offer
as well as receive from the education service in their area.
This will become more and more important as the number
of elderly, but healthy and experienced, people grows in
proportion to the rest of the population.

Another feature of a recurrent strategy, which the adult
literacy campaign displayed to the nation, was the importance of professional partnerships, both within the field of
education and across educational boundaries. Not only were
radio, television and the press widely used to publicize the
scheme and to recruit students, but libraries, shops,
museums, doctors, social services, milkmen, postmen and
many other agencies and individuals were also used to communicate with potential students. This local collaboration
and partnership is a feature of adult education networks, and
the way in which new ideas and projects are created as well
as disseminated. There may be few opportunities again for
such a nationwide project as the adult literacy campaign,
but there will always be reasons locally for fostering professional partnerships. And the model now exists, because of
adult literacy, for an on-going relationship between the central authority and the local, front-line education centres. One
can imagine one or two government-sponsored and locally
administered adult education projects in the future, run on
similar lines to the literacy campaign, perhaps in health
education, or women's education, or education for retirement. One negative benefit of adult literacy was to show up

those local education authorities which had failed to develop, or had run down, their adult education services, thereby rendering them unable to respond to such a clear-cut need.

Perhaps the most significant and optimistic feature of the entire adult literacy campaign is its continuing follow-up, and its development as an integral part of the wider concept of adult basic education (ABE). There was perhaps a danger that the whole scheme might have been a 'one-off' event, an admirable pilot project which, like so many others in the history of adult education, never took off to become part of the broad and continuing national movement. But ABE looks as though it will provide a permanent conceptual and administrative framework within which local centres will be able to choose the most appropriate way to meet the basic learning needs of a large sector of their local adult population.

The roots of ABE lie very firmly in the literacy scheme. It quickly became apparent to many sensitive organizers and tutors working on literacy projects that a number of their students had more generalized learning problems than those relating specifically to reading and writing. Often found were problems of simple arithmetic and number work, and many areas in consequence have established numeracy schemes. But there were also problems related to self-confidence and the individual's incapacity to manage simple aspects of daily life; many adults lack social and communication skills of a basic kind. But they can be helped to acquire them. By considering the possibility, at least, of providing for these 'life skills,' alongside help with specific literacy and numeracy problems, adult educators are in a position to devise or to call on a greater variety of educational solutions to the particular problems of each individual student. ABE is an example of 'raising the level of aggregation' in education. While literacy, numeracy and other specific learning areas like 'English as a Foreign Language' remain crucial in themselves, they can only benefit from being seen in the more general perspective of ABE.

ABE is one of the major concerns of the Advisory Council for Adult and Continuing Education (ACACE) which after much pressure was set up by the Labour Government in 1977.[23] Although in part a direct result of the Russell Committee Report which asked in 1973 for a National Development Council for adult education, ACACE has taken a step further on the path to recurrent education in Britain. Unlike the Russell Committee, its terms of reference do not restrict it to 'non-vocational education'. Indeed, the second of its two terms of reference empowers ACACE 'to promote the development of future policies and priorities with full regard to the concept of education as a process continuing throughout life'.[24] ACACE is aiming to publish in 1980 a report on 'what a continuing education system of provision might look like in 1990 and in 2000'.[25] If the 1980s should see government intervention which moves Britain in the directions discussed in this book, it is likely that ACACE will be one of the most influential pressure groups bringing it about.

We have not attempted to look in detail at what such new statutes might contain. Clearly, new legislation will be necessary if recurrent education is to emerge as a total strategy for British education. Issues which need legislation include: the age of entry to, and departure from, compulsory child education; the fundamental right of all adults to education and, where applicable, to paid educational leave; the divisions of responsibility between national education and training departments; the nature of the relationship between the central government's authority and the local education authorities; and, more precisely, the differing roles and responsibilities of central, regional, local and institutional authorities. But the way ahead cannot be imposed by law. Legislation has to wait for public attitudes and the 'pressure of the times'. ACACE is in a position to hasten both the government's and the public's understanding of the different emphases and implications of recurrent education.

Distance Learning: Correspondence Education and Broadcasting

The phrases 'distance learning' or 'education at a distance' embrace both correspondence courses and the formal educational programmes offered on radio and television. Its most fruitful forms are those educational ventures, like the Open University, which combine both correspondence course work and broadcasts. Especially interesting, in the context of this chapter, are those collaborative projects which also involve established educational institutions, not just as meeting-places for home-based students but as equal partners in the entire task of planning, tutoring and assessing their work. A diverse recurrent education system, with the accent on individualized programmes of study from adolescence onwards, must rely heavily on materials which emanate outside educational institutions, with their limited human resources. Correspondence colleges and the broadcasting organizations can provide a great variety of learning aids and stimuli, of potential value to all students whether they are primarily home or college-based. Just as today many full-time university students find the Open University material valuable (and so do their teachers), so eventually might all students at all ability levels be able to use appropriate distance-learning material, and to adapt it, with tutorial assistance from their local education centres, to their particular learning requirements.

The old image of correspondence education as dull provision, incompetently taught and unscrupulously administered, is breaking down, and not just because of the Open University's success. Other educational organizations have recognized that the pattern developed by the Open University – written and broadcast material leading to assignments in the home, interspersed with periodic tutorial guidance and with group learning outside the home – is only one model for distance study, and one which is capable of much variation. Where there is a willingness to co-operate and to experiment within existing institutions, there is no need to create new, large-scale organizations like the Open University.

The National Extension College (NEC) has developed links with many further education colleges and adult education centres, and has shown the potential significance of distant study methods for diversity and individual attention in a recurrent system. Acting on the two principles that almost anything can be taught at a distance, given imagination in course design, but that, however highly motivated, home-based students nearly always need support, the NEC has worked to create not just attractive courses in many subjects but also a network of local study centres where students can find support.[26] In conjunction with Barnet College of Further Education it has created a 'Flexistudy' scheme which places distance learning methods right in the heart of the college's own provision. Students are entitled to a specific number of hours with a tutor of the college, who marks assignments and generally follows the student's progress. The students have all the advantages of being students of Barnet College, but by using NEC materials they are able to do most of their work in their own time at home. Wherever they live, whatever their work or other constraining activities, they can be college students receiving individual help with their chosen courses. These courses can start at any time of the year; the students can attend tutorials at any agreed time of the week; the range of courses offered can include minority subjects which would not be financially viable in the traditional class format.[27] These are the advantages of distance learning.

It is too early to say that the words 'college' and 'education' no longer conjure up an automatic picture of groups of students in classrooms, but the seeds of a more individualized image of education can be found in the Flexistudy scheme. The Oxbridge tutorial system with its concentration on individual tuition has long shown to a narrow range of people, and in an expensive way, that the classroom and the group are only two possible ingredients of an educational process. Through distance-learning methods the tutorial method is capable of a much wider application, and of being implemented at much less cost.

The National Extension College has been associated with many other distance-learning projects in recent years. These include the Open College idea pioneered in Lancashire and the North-west, cited in the previous chapter as an exciting development in the field of community education. Enough has been achieved to make a national system of learning based on distant study principles a practicable proposition Two NEC projects in the late 1970s have suggested how television might be used in such a system. One, in conjunction with Westward Television, was designed for unemployed school-leavers, and it used the adult literacy model of networks of support, created by professional educators and manned by volunteers; the other, in conjunction with Yorkshire Television, was created for adult numeracy students.[28] The scope of education at a distance extends from the most basic educational level to the most advanced graduate research. The next stage must be to ensure that, where appropriate, the three key elements of the provision – correspondence materials, college tutors and broadcasting agencies – are brought together in a continuing and permanent partnership, and not just for specific and sporadic projects.

Both the BBC and ITV have also for many years been initiating their own educational projects for school pupils and for adults. Books, tapes or records are usually produced to supplement and follow up the broadcasts. In adult education, successful subjects have included special O-level courses (*Living Decisions* and *What Rights Have You Got?*), trade-union studies, foreign languages, yoga and cookery. In general, educational broadcasting is most effective when there is prior consultation and collaboration with educational organizations, whether these are schools, or colleges, or adult education centres, or even, in the case of the two O levels above, examination boards. The broadcasts and associated books and materials, however excellent in themselves, can seldom provide a complete educational process. Home-based students of foreign languages, for example, must practise their conversation skills on other people. Broadcasting on television and radio provided tremendous advertising and a useful referral service for the adult literacy campaign; but alone it could not hope to provide all the course work, follow-up and continuous help necessary to achieve progress in reading and writing skills. Even in yoga and cookery, most students need a human contact to assist them, to monitor their progress and to ensure that learning is effectively taking place and in the right direction. Television and radio programmes, and associated material, are only in exceptional cases sufficient by themselves to provide genuinely educational processes. It may well be that the future development of PRESTEL and similar systems, by which individuals can call up information for display on their television sets, will allow the creation of interactive learning programmes. But that is in the future.

A recurrent education strategy has to avoid the enticing notion which equates education with any and all communication. It is naïve, for example, to assume that any particular television programme or series, whether labelled as an educational broadcast or not, is having an educational effect in the home. Education must involve a conscious choice by students to take part in it, and to step aside from their normal routines of living (like watching television) in order to do so. The powerful arguments for improving society's major communication outlets, for making truthful television documentaries, or for putting agricultural tips into *The Archers*, must not be confused with the case for recurrent education.[29] In a civilized society they are both important. But they are separate, and when confused the *reductio ad absurdum* is quickly reached, which states that all life is education and vice versa.

Counselling, Guidance and Information Services

In practice, a recurrent system of education will stand or fall by the quality of the counselling, guidance and information services which are available to help students make their choices. In recurrent education terms, counselling is not offering advice about the best schools in an area, nor on how to assert parental rights. It is the fundamental, lifelong process of advising and accompanying individual students so that they can use the education system, to help them achieve their personal development goals, and to help them adjust to the various social challenges which face them.

Even in today's restricted adult education sector, there are sufficiently numerous educational opportunities for many people to have been persuaded of the need for counselling and information services. At local level a number of schemes are in operation. At the time of writing, two of the largest schemes are in Sheffield and in South Glamorgan. The Sheffield Adult Education Information and Survey Project is working simultaneously on several strands of a counselling service.[30] It sees the need to inform potential students directly, through established institutions of adult, further and higher education, through mobile 'clinics' manned by counsellors, and through other public information outlets such as libraries, shops, cinemas, and so on. It has suggested a need for a register of educational opportunities which can be immediately comprehended by potential adult students. But the project has also emphasized the importance of keeping the professionals and providers of education up to date with accurate information, so that they, too, can inform and guide potential students. Finally, the project has established the desirability of training a team of counsellors, who might be professional full-timers, or paid part-timers or, not least, volunteers.

The South Glamorgan educational resources and information centre (ERIC), funded by the Manpower Services

Commission as a result of the Open University's initial request, is in some ways an even more ambitious scheme than the Sheffield project. Its computer-based information bank seeks to ensure that information about courses in the area is constantly up to date. As well as providing information services and guidance both for students and for professionals, it has two more objectives: 'to research un-met adult education needs' and 'to facilitate greater contact between educational providers as to the demand for information and the likely demand for courses'.[31] Both the Sheffield and the South Glamorgan schemes are in an early stage of their development. But it is already apparent that the teaching and administrative components of a total educational service will be inseparable from a large-scale counselling component.

We have suggested in this chapter that the future, or way ahead, in British education is being approached from many different directions. The educational present contains within it the seeds of the educational future. But there can be no certainty that the fragments outlined above will ever be pieced together in a co-ordinated framework of recurrent education. The forces of inertia, vested interest and entrenched attitude, discussed in Chapters 4 and 5, as well as short-term political calculations, could keep the British public's notion of education firmly associated with childhood. The way to overcome these forces is to emphasize an evolutionary approach to the creation of a recurrent system. A new education system will emerge through the use of rational argument and gentle persuasion, and through those individual initiatives which build up new links, new networks and new attitudes. The recurrent education themes in this book both arise from and depend on such an approach to change. We have tried to depict the features of the changes which might appear, but such features will never be static. The themes restated in the final paragraph are not proposals for a single reform, or set of reforms, in British education;

they are guidelines for continuing educational growth and change at all levels of educational policy-making and practice.

An education system must provide lifelong and life-wide opportunities for learning. An education system must operate as a whole system, incorporating both the compulsory education of the young and the educational rights of the old. An education system must itself be a learning system, able to respond flexibly to individual and social need, and therefore able to change itself from within.

References

1 B. Crowe, *The Playgroup Movement*, 3rd edn, London, George Allen & Unwin, 1977.
2 Department of Education and Science, *Children and their Primary Schools* (The Plowden Report), London, HMSO, 1967, p. 469.
3 *A New Partnership for our Schools* (see note 26 to Chapter 4).
4 Report by Joan Sallis, the *Guardian*, 14 November 1978, p. 19.
5 *School/Industry Liaison – A Guide for Teachers,* UBI, Sun Alliance House, New Inn Hall Street, Oxford.
6 Account in the *Guardian*, 6 July 1978, p. 16.
7 But the PEL Project Report is due in 1979–80 (see note 4 to Chapter 6).
8 *Assessment – Why, What and How?*, APU, Second Information Leaflet, 1977.
9 *Unified Vocational Preparation – A Pilot Approach*, p. 3 (see note 25 to Chapter 5).
10 Further Education Curriculum Review and Development Unit, *Experience, Reflection, Learning*, 1978, p. 35.
11 *Unified Vocational Preparation – A Pilot Approach*, p. 7 (see note 25 to Chapter 5).
12 Engineering Industrial Training Board Information Paper No. 49, March 1978.

13 Lindsay, *Social Progress and Educational Waste* (see note 11 to Chapter 5).

14 A Policy Statement by the Technician Education Council, June 1974, p. 9.

15 *Educational Credit Transfer: Feasibility Study*, Project Director, P. Toyne, Hailey Wing, Reed Hall, Exeter University, Exeter EX4 4QR.

16 C. Ellwood, *Adult Learning Today. A New Role for the Universities*, SAGE Publications Ltd, 1976.

17 Report by C. Griffin-Beale, the *Guardian*, 21 November 1978, p. 11.

18 Burgess, *Education after School*, p. 159 (see note 24 to Chapter 4).

19 R. Hoggart, *After Expansion: A Time for Diversity* ACACE, 1978, p. 9.

20 The Venables Report, p. 28 (see note 15 to Chapter 6).

21 H. A. Jones, and A. H. Charnley *Adult Literacy: A Study of its Impact*, National Institute for Adult Education, 1978.

22 *Learning Exchange – The Idea in Practice,* a resource pack compiled by the Board for Information on Youth and Community Service, 67 York Place, Edinburgh, EH1 3JD.

23 Statement by the Department of Education and Science, 18 October 1977.

24 Ibid.

25 Advisory Council for Adult and Continuing Education, Information Release No. 8, 13 October 1978.

26 *Study Centre Guide*, National Extension College, Local Centres' Booklet, 1977.

27 *Flexistudy – A Manual for Local Colleges*, Barnet College of Further Education, National Extension College Reports, Series 2, No. 4, 1978.

28 'Just the Job' and 'Make it Count'.

29 For a discussion of this issue and a different view, see D. Anderson, 'Continuing Education and the Future of Broadcasting', *Adult Education,* vol. 48, no. 3, September 1975, pp. 170–8.

30 *Sheffield Adult Education Information and Survey Project, January–September 1977.* See also A. W. Bacon, 'An

Educational Advisory Service for Adults', *Social Services Quarterly*, vol. II, no. 1, July–September 1977, p. 10.

31   S. Murgatroyd and A. Patterson, 'An Educational Resources Information Centre (ERIC)', *Adult Education*, vol. 51, no. 1. May 1978, p. 31. Unfortunately ERIC was forced to close its operation in March 1979 owing to lack of money.

174

176